The Art of
Stitching on Metal

ANN PARR

SEARCH PRESS

First published in Great Britain 2008

Search Press Limited
Wellwood, North Farm Road,
Tunbridge Wells, Kent TN2 3DR

Reprinted 2009

Text copyright © Ann Parr 2008

Photographs by Roddy Paine Photographic Studios

Photographs and design copyright © Search Press Ltd. 2008

ISBN: 978 1 84448 225 2

The Publishers and author can accept no responsibility for any
consequences arising from the information, advice or instructions
given in this publication.

Suppliers
If you have difficulty in obtaining any of the materials and equipment
mentioned in this book, then please visit the Search Press website:
www.searchpress.com for a current list of stockists, including firms
who operate a mail-order service.

Publishers' note

All the step-by-step photographs in this book feature the
author, Ann Parr, demonstrating stitching on metal. No
models have been used.

All of the details provided for the materials described on
page 12 were found to be correct at the time of writing.

Images on pages 2 and 3

*Hand-made felt had strips of dyed muslin embedded in it during
the felting process. As the felt shrank the muslin became ruched.
Scraps of fabric were free machined on to a cold-water-soluble
film which was then dissolved and the resulting fabric cut into
strips. Small pieces of copper shim were attached at intervals to
the strips and these were machined down on to the felt, leaving
four small gaps between each piece of copper shim. Cords of wire
and threads were wrapped around the strips through the gaps
and tied, with the ends bent down.*

Image shown opposite (page 5)

*This metal sampler has a heat-treated brass wire mesh
background showing items in copper shim and copper foil,
influenced by the designs of the tapa cloths of
the Pacific.*

Dedication

*This book is dedicated to my husband Geoff, for
all his love and support in everything I do; my
daughter Jane and her husband Ed; my son David
and his wife Tanya; my son Dan and his wife Jo;
and my grandchildren Emilia, Meredith, Conrad,
Harry, Seb, Bethan and Archie.*

Acknowledgements

*I would like to thank everyone at Search
Press, especially Katie, Roz, Juan, Ellie and
photographers Roddy and Gavin, without whom
this book could not have been produced.*

*I would also like to thank Pam Watts for her
constant support. She has fostered my love of
machine embroidery and encouraged me to write
this book.*

*My grateful thanks also to Chris Burrows for her
help with the computer.*

*This box is made of copper decorated with stitching and glass
paints and is lined with decorative automatic machine stitching on
yellow silk. It has been kindly loaned for illustration in this book by
Mrs Barbara Willis.*

Contents

Introduction

The variety of results that can be achieved when working with metals and the traditional materials used in creative textile work is quite astonishing. With the wide range of metal forms now available, for example fine metallic woven cloth, metal shim and foil, wire mesh and enamelled wire, there seems to be no limit to the wonderful decorative objects that can be produced.

The colour of some of these metals can be changed by heating and, with the addition of everyday products used in the kitchen or garden, the colours can be further enriched. The metals can also be painted, foiled, embossed and stitched, and decorated using various types of fusible webs and puff paints. Experiments can be carried out using any combination of the above treatments and often some unique and spectacular results are achieved.

The methods and techniques used in this book will produce successful results. However, when heating metal and treating with chemicals it is impossible to reproduce exactly the same results each time. Do not be surprised if your work varies in colour or texture from the effect you were aiming for. Experiments using different methods and techniques make working with metals extremely exciting. Happily, sometimes when something may appear to have 'gone wrong' you might even achieve a better result than that intended.

As you would with traditional embroidery, use a sketchbook to record designs seen in museums, exhibitions, ethnic and historical embroideries, parks and gardens. Shapes such as grids, squares, circles and patches have appeared in designs for centuries in many cultures and these can be used very successfully when embossing metals. Record the results of your experiments in a separate book, detailing the method and materials used; in this way you will always have available the manner in which you have achieved a particular effect.

Treated or untreated metal can be used purely as a background for a piece of work and it can also be used as small patches for embellishments or, as with the pewter boxes and pendants on pages 68 to 77, stitched to change the appearance.

For a beginner, stitching into metal using a sewing machine may seem to be a rather violent and dangerous exercise but both machine stitching and hand stitching can be achieved quite easily, especially with the thin and malleable metals now available. There are a number of metals that can be used – copper, brass, aluminium, stainless steel, copper wire mesh, brass wire mesh, pewter, woven metal cloth and also the recycled soft metallic tubes used to contain such products as tomato, garlic and onion purée. When these metallic tubes are cut open and washed, they are ideal to use particularly for practice but, unlike the copper and brass shims and foils, they do not respond in the same way to heat. The metal from this source will darken and appear richer in colour but when heating copper and brass there are dramatic changes in colour – red, blue, silver and orange.

6

Chatelaine

The mistress of a castle was known as the chatelaine, but it is also the name given to a chain or clasp worn at the waist by women in the sixteenth to nineteenth centuries with useful items attached, such as a purse, a watch, keys, a book, scissors and a perfume bottle.

Research for this chatelaine was carried out at the Victoria and Albert Museum in London. To simulate filigree silver, it is made of pewter on a bump backing with free machining using silver metallic thread. All the items are workable except for the watch case.

Patina antiquing agents, acrylic paints, glass paints, metallic paints, foils, dyes, inks and embossing powders, used after colour changes achieved by heating, can further enhance the colour change. Embossing and stitching will complete the transformation.

Metal can be used in the same way as fabric as a backing for a decorative surface such as fusible mesh, webs and puff paints. These can all be coloured and applied with stitch to metal and can then be heated to change their appearance. Alternatively a design of free machining on water-soluble film can be placed on metal with only a rare, shining glimpse of the background metal showing through. Stitching on pewter brings particularly spectacular results as it can simulate filigree silver which can be used for jewellery and decorative three-dimensional items.

Details and illustrations are shown in the early sections of this book enabling you to see the results of these different treatments. Do your own experiments and you will achieve many wonderful and varied results. Be encouraged to delve into the stitching of metal and to pursue your own projects.

In the following chapters I hope to take you on a journey of discovery; you will learn to prepare metals, decorate them, stitch them and achieve many original pieces of work ranging from jewellery, boxes, book covers and cards, to metal dolls and even a metal 'sampler'. I hope you will be stimulated by the contents of this book and acquire the knowledge and enthusiasm to produce original and interesting work.

Chatelaine (detail)
12 x 4.7cm (4¾ x 1¾in)

This panel hangs from the waist fastening, and from the base five cords are suspended. On the ends of these cords are the five items most often used by the owner of the chatelaine.

Chatelaine (detail)
5 x 4.2cm (2 x 1¾in)

This book has stitched pewter covers with cartridge paper signatures and is made using the coptic stitch. The book has a fastening of fine wire cords fitted into the edge of both covers, one with a loop and the other with a small bugle bead to thread through the loop.

Chatelaine (detail)
Diameter 5.5cm (2¼in)

Two decoratively stitched circles of pewter are padded with layers of bump to a depth suitable to contain a watch. The size of the watchcase had to be in keeping with the other four items but unfortunately I could not find a watch of a suitable size to use to make this a workable item.

Materials

The use of metals in textiles was first recorded thousands of years ago and these techniques are still used today, particularly in the East. A visit to any museum displaying Eastern textiles will give you some wonderful examples.

An initial use of metal in your work in a minor way will no doubt inspire you to experiment with other types of metal. The metals most readily available and also the most reliable for stitching are copper, pewter, brass and aluminium. The thickness of metal sheeting, wire mesh and metallic woven cloth varies but it obviously needs to be thin enough to be stitched with a sewing machine or by hand.

Sumptuous materials such as velvets, chiffons and silks used to line three-dimensional objects are the perfect complement to metal. They can also be used as a decorative background on which to display metal designs. There are many decorative surface finishes available now, such as fusible webbing and puff paint, which can be coloured, stitched or heated to alter their appearance.

The variety of threads and cords is endless and encourages compulsive buying – there is always another thread you must have! Wire has many uses and some of these will be covered later in this book.

Metals

The metals referred to in this book come in the form of shim, foil, wire mesh and woven cloth. The thickness can vary depending on the metal and the supplier, but copper shim at 0.12mm (0.005in) is considered to be about the thickest that is acceptable to use with a sewing machine.

Copper comes from various metal suppliers in rolls, or from art and craft suppliers in small packs (or 'taster' packs) of assorted metals. Rolls of adhesive-backed metal tapes are available in various widths. Ultra-fine woven cloth at 0.012mm (0.0005in) thickness has a wonderful gossamer-like appearance, shim at 0.15mm (0.006in) thickness is a comfortable thickness to work with and foil at 0.06mm (0.002in) or thinner needs careful handling.

There is a copper foil available which has a matt side and a polished side. It is the matt side which shows dramatic changes when heat-treated and adds an almost medieval effect to your work, especially when used in conjunction with other subtly coloured fabrics as shown on page 51.

Pewter, used to simulate filigree silver, is heavier than copper but is soft and malleable and a joy to stitch on the sewing machine. It can be torn as well as cut with a craft knife or craft scissors and is available in rolls and small packs.

Aluminium is available in rolls, sheets or 'taster' packs in different colours or textures and in thicknesses of up to 0.3mm (0.01in) for embossing.

Brass, a mixture of copper and zinc, varies in colour depending on the balance of these two constituents. Different suppliers will have a different balance which will affect the colour and reaction when the metal is treated with heat. An ideal thickness would be about 0.12mm (0.005in).

Woven fabrics sold as wire mesh or as a delicate, woven metal cloth are available in various weights depending upon the thread count. It is unusual to find the relevant information on the 'taster' packs but wire mesh is usually thicker and heavier than woven metal cloth, which can be almost gossamer thin. The fine woven cloths have many uses and can be heat-treated and scrunched, rolled, folded, cut into strips and used as ribbon edges.

Machine-knitted wires are sold as knitted wire tubes available in a range of colours and diameters and can be used in jewellery and embellishments. They are very versatile as they can be twisted and scrunched into various shapes.

Food containers such as tomato and garlic paste tubes are useful when cleaned as they react in a different way to heat treatment. Drink cans can also be used, with the outer coloured designs producing interesting effects to the finished work.

Dense stainless steel mesh, as used in commercial filter coffee jugs, is not readily available but has interesting properties.

Untreated metals

Most of the examples of untreated metals shown on the following pages (pages 14 to 15) are readily available and a number of them have been used in this book.

Untreated metal samples

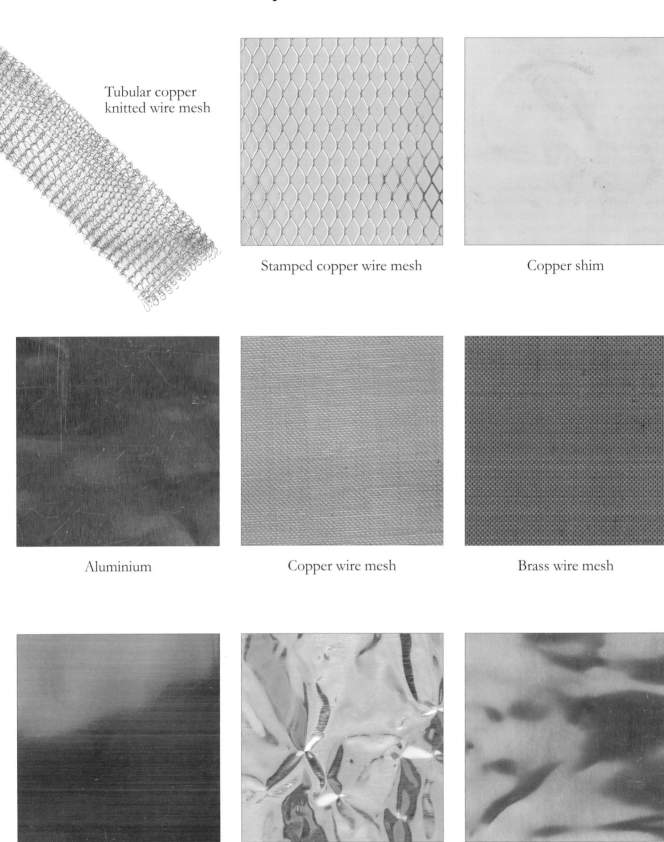

Tubular copper
knitted wire mesh

Stamped copper wire mesh

Copper shim

Aluminium

Copper wire mesh

Brass wire mesh

Brass shim

Light-weight pewter

Pewter

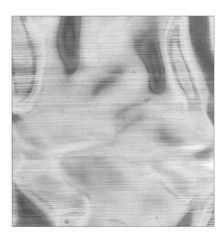

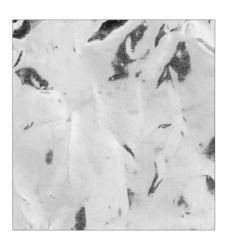

Copper foil, polished side

Copper foil, matt side

Fine woven copper cloth

Stainless steel woven mesh

Fine stainless steel woven cloth

Very fine copper foil

Painted aluminium

Copper woven cloth

Tomato purée tube

Fabrics and finishes

Almost any material can be used when stitching with metal; not only the traditional fabrics of velvet, silk, chiffon, furnishing fabric and Vilene (craft interfacing) but also leather, plastic and even balsa wood.

Decorative and lining fabrics

Sumptuous fabrics can be used with metals in many ways. They can provide a beautiful lining for a three-dimensional object such as a box or, combined with a fabric such as Angelina, they can offer an exciting background on which to display metal decoration. Angelina fibres are obtainable in small quantities in bags of different colours and when ironed between sheets of baking parchment they are transformed into delicate sheets of fabric. The colours can be mixed and threads can be added to the fibres before heating.

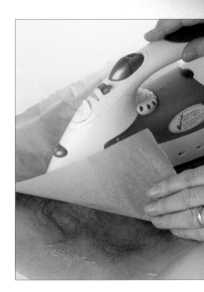

Making Angelina sheets.

Yellow silk, which has been decorated with an automatic decorative machine embroidery stitch and is the lining for the box on page 4.

Silk rods can be soaked in water and thin layers peeled off for use, as in the embroidered cuff on page 90.

Backing fabrics

It is useful to have a backing fabric to give stability to the metal when stitching by hand or machine. Backing fabrics also facilitate the use of metal when machine stitching by enabling the punctured metal edges to 'bed down' into a soft fabric, thereby reducing the risk of the sewing thread shredding. When stitching pewter to achieve a filigree effect, the machine needle makes quite a large hole in the metal and the backing fabric therefore plays an important role in avoiding shredding of the thread. It also prevents the bed of the sewing machine from being scratched. In some cases a backing fabric is not essential, such as when stitching wire mesh, woven metal cloth and some of the shims.

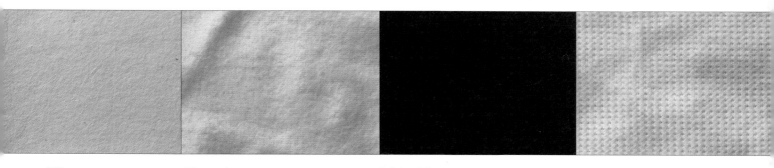

Vilene

Vilene is an interfacing. It is available in a number of thicknesses but the craft weight is the most acceptable and versatile when stitching with metal.

Flannelette

Thick flannelette is a traditional fabric and is a cotton imitation of flannel. Old flannelette bed sheets can be recycled but they do not provide quite the same stability as the other backing fabrics.

Thin felt

Felt is an extremely versatile backing fabric and is available in a number of thicknesses and colours. Kunin felt is an acrylic felt with added polyester, which enables it to distress when heated.

Bump

Bump is a curtain interlining which hangs between the curtain fabric and the lining. It provides additional warmth and protection from winter draughts and makes an excellent backing when stitching with metal.

Velvet has been used for the background of this panel with adhesive powder sprinkled on and foil ironed over it. Layers of purple-dyed silk rods were placed over the top and machine stitched down the centre of each to keep them in place. A layer of black chiffon was laid on the top and was randomly free machine stitched using a dark thread. A heat gun was then used to partially disintegrate the chiffon. This decorative, textured background can be used for displaying metal patches or knitted wire squares, etc.

A background of black felt was used for this sample with a sheet of very fine copper foil placed on top. A sheet of Angelina made from a number of different coloured fibres was placed on top followed by two layers of black chiffon. The sandwich was machine stitched around the edges and a few horizontal and vertical lines were machine stitched to hold everything in place. The chiffon was then heated with a heat gun to distress the surface. This background was used for the woven panel shown on pages 98–101.

Decorative surface finishes

Decorative surface finishes such as fusible webbing or mesh, fusible fibres, puff paints (dimension paints that give a raised surface when dry), etc. add texture and colour to metal. The soluble films and papers also enable stitch and fabric to be incorporated into the decoration of metal. To protect surfaces when applying these finishes, remember to have parchment paper on the ironing board and over the product before heating with an iron.

Tyvek

A fabric created from high-density polyethylene. It is non-toxic and can shrink and bubble when heated. It can also be coloured before or after heating. Stitching takes place before heating.

Fibretex

Similar to Tyvek but is soft and fibre-like. It can also be coloured, stitched and heated.

Sizoflor

A webbing which is available in a number of colours. It can be stitched and also heated to change the appearance.

Bondaweb

A soft, fusible adhesive mesh attached to greaseproof paper. It can bond two fabrics together and also bond with metal. It can be coloured with paints, inks and dyes.

Garden fleece

A fine web used to protect delicate plants, but it can also be used as a fusible web which can be painted and heated to distort its appearance.

FuseFX

A gossamer bonding mesh which takes colour and gives a webbed effect when applied to metal with an iron. It is also available in black.

Lutradur

A non-woven synthetic material which is available in at least four weights. You should wear a respirator mask when heating this material.

Aquabond

A water-soluble adhesive backed with paper which peels off and enables your work to be held in place. It is then covered with another layer of water-soluble film before stitching and is removed with water.

Water-soluble paper

A stabiliser for machine embroidery and can be drawn on. It can be washed away completely, or used as part of the decoration when only partially washed away. It can also be used when damp to take a mould from a printing block, as shown on page 55.

Water-soluble film

A light-weight stabiliser for machine embroidery which can then be washed away.

Magic Film and Tricky Film

Fine removable films for use as a backing for machine embroidery. They can be stitched and the film removed with an iron or heat gun.

Thermogaze

Sometimes called Thermogauze or vanishing muslin, this is a firm, heat-sensitive vanishing fabric which can be stitched and then dispersed with heat from a dry iron, a heat gun or by putting a large piece in a tumble dryer.

Painted Lutradur 30 with a printing block design stamped on. It is possible to see the fibres more clearly after painting.

A piece of copper foil was ribbled (see page 40) then Fibretex, painted green, was placed over the copper foil and gently heated. The Fibretex distressed and adhered to the copper.

Painted Lutradur 30 was placed on a copper foil background. A grid was stitched over the two layers and flowers stitched in each square. It was then heat-treated.

Painted Lutradur 70 was free machine stitched in a floral design on to heat-treated brass wire mesh, then heated with a craft heat gun to distort the surface.

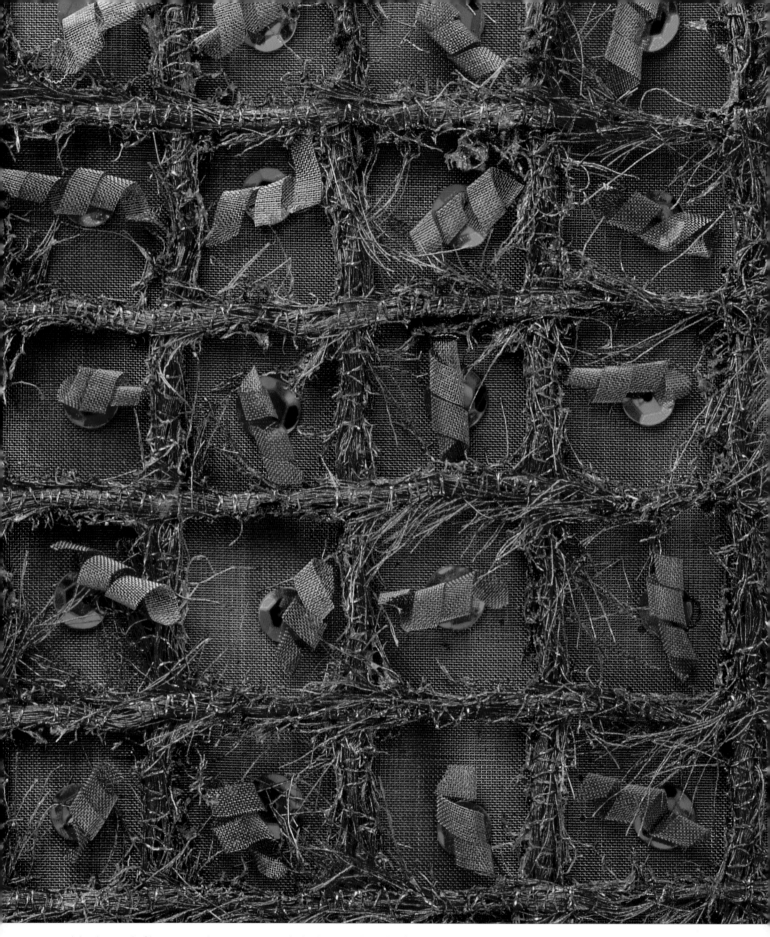

A background of heat-treated copper wire mesh displays a grid made of a decorative
fluffy cord. This cord was made using a decorative Christmas cord into which wire was
incorporated, and then the two were free machine stitched together with a zig-zag stitch.
A pink sequin with a curl of heat-treated wire mesh was stitched by hand into each square.

Wires and threads

Wires

Wire is available in many thicknesses and colours; the thicker the wire, the lower the gauge number. It can be knitted, crocheted, stitched over with a zig-zag stitch on the sewing machine to make a cord, incorporated in three-dimensional items, wrapped around objects, or made into beads. Thicknesses suitable for knitting are 30g, 32g and 34g, but 26g and 28g can be knitted and give a more solid structure. The thicker wires, 18g to 22g, can give support but not in a knitted form.

The photograph below illustrates the various ways in which wires can be bought, from small quantities wound in a circle to large, industrial-sized bobbins of copper and enamelled copper.

Machine embroidery threads

Almost any machine embroidery thread can be used when stitching metal, although some are more user-friendly than others. Metallic threads are more likely to shred than a plain sewing thread but it is always a good idea to experiment first on a small piece of metal. Fine silver metallic thread free machine stitched into pewter with a soft fabric backing achieves an excellent result.

Decorative threads

Any three or four of the threads shown in this photograph could be used to create a cord for edging three-dimensional items, such as those used in making the pewter boxes on page 74. The cord could also incorporate wire when it is required to hold a shape, as on page 87 (the seedhead vessel). The choice of threads is endless and varies between fine and smooth; chunky and thick; thin ribbon yarn; knitting yarn; metallic threads for hand sewing; wool; synthetic fibres; silks; and strands of embroidery silks – and, of course, the colours available are wonderful. The embroiderer can never have enough threads and we are seduced by the range available.

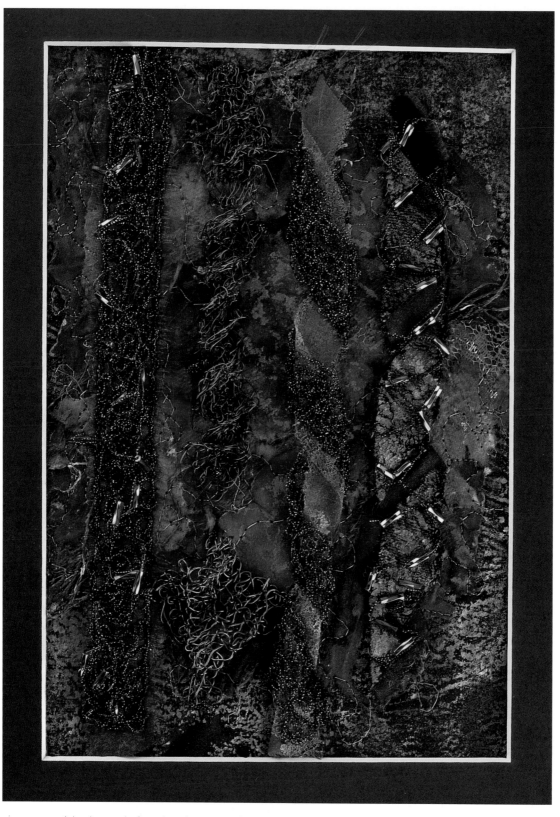

A background of purple velvet, treated with painted Bondaweb (fusible adhesive mesh), had pieces of painted hand-made paper randomly stitched in place. Twisted and wrapped decorative strips were then applied. From left to right, these are: a strip of free machining on water-soluble film, which was wound with beaded, wrapped (stitched) wire and then applied by hand; a strip of knitted wire, twisted and applied by hand; painted Bondaweb applied to a fine gauze with a strip of free machining on water-soluble film on top, and the layers twisted and applied by hand; a strip of painted Bondaweb applied to velvet, twisted, and with a beaded and wrapped (stitched) wire wound around it in two directions.

Decorating the metal

A fascinating technique for changing the appearance of metal is the application of heat, particularly to copper and, to a lesser extent, to brass. Applying heat and watching the colour change run across the sheet of metal is very exciting. Learning to control the amount of heat needed to change the colour requires a few practice runs. Probably the ultimate heating experience is to heat copper until it is red hot, then to place it straight into a bowl of water. The result is a rich dark red and a suggestion of other dark colours. After heating, copper and brass can be treated with corrosive substances such as lemon juice, vinegar, bleach, salt and ammonia (see page 34). However, if copper and brass are first soaked in balsamic vinegar and then heated there is a deeper colour reaction. Art and craft shops can supply rust activators and patina antiquing agents which will produce yet another effect when applied to copper.

Adding texture is another way of decorating the metal prior to stitching. This can be achieved by a variety of methods. Embossing can be carried out with an old biro (containing no ink), embossing tools, a pastry wheel, a dress-making pin wheel, paper ribblers (crimpers) or a commercial embossing stamp.

Opposite: A detail of the panel shown on page 45.

Left: crumpled, heat-treated matt copper was painted with Pebeo puff paint following the outline of the design created by the heat treatment. Black polish was applied with a finger over the surface of the creases and the paint outline.

Basic equipment

Many items of equipment needed when treating metal can be found in the home. Look at your kitchen utensils; you may find some tools which would make some unusual marks on metal not covered by any of the items shown here or on page 39.

A chef's blow torch is an efficient source of heat as it can be used in any location, unlike the gas cooker! The heat is easily controlled, increasing in intensity by a slight turn of the cap on the top. A variety of heat guns can be obtained from any art and craft shop but there is a difference between them in the intensity of heat produced. The most efficient heat gun when heating metal is one of at least 360W. DIY paint-stripper heat guns are really too powerful. Some embossing heat guns are not powerful enough to achieve a significant change in the colour of the copper and brass or to effect the required change in surface-decoration materials. Other heat sources include candles and tea lights so matches will also be required. The heat travels very quickly along a piece of metal, so never pick up a piece of newly heated metal with bare hands and always hold the metal in a pair of tongs while heating.

There are various corrosive substances that can be used to treat the metal once it has been heated, for example salt, bleach, lemon juice, methylated spirits, ammonia and balsamic vinegar. Always wear protective gloves when handling these substances and a respirator mask when using ammonia, bleach and patina antiquing agents. To contain the liquids you will need a variety of plastic trays, for example a cat litter tray and various plastic food containers, and a roll of small, clear plastic food bags. Keep a roll of absorbent paper to hand for mopping up the inevitable spills.

Baking parchment and an iron are needed when applying various decorative surface finishes (see page 20) and for making Angelina sheets (see page 16). You will also need a craft knife, a metal ruler and various pairs of scissors for different purposes. Good quality dress-making scissors are required for cutting fabrics; also a pair of scissors used only for cutting paper (as paper blunts scissors), an old pair of scissors for cutting metal, and craft scissors with a decorative edge to the blades for cutting decorative edges on metal, card or paper.

Strong, clear all-purpose glue, double-sided adhesive tape, PVA glue and masking tape are used in some of the projects in this book. Tracing paper and a selection of pencils are necessary when a design is traced for embossing on the metal.

Heating metal

Holding the piece of metal in a pair of **wet***, long-handled bamboo tweezers, move the metal over the heat source and watch carefully as the heat and colour travel across the metal. If it is held 2cm (1in) from the heat source, it will change colour quickly. The metal shown here is the matt side of copper foil. Experiment with the distance and change the heat source and the metals used, and you will soon gain confidence and skill.*

Heating

Different ways of applying heat will have varied effects on the range of metals shown here. Sources of heat can be gas cookers, electric hotplates, powerful craft heat guns, a cook's blow torch, a candle or a tea light. The source of the metal, its weight, and the duration and intensity of heat are all factors to be considered when heating metal. It is recommended that a sample book (see page 36) be used to record experiments with all the relevant details listed. It must be stressed that there is no guarantee you will be able to reproduce any piece exactly, but with a record in your sample book of the methods previously used you will at least have information to refer to.

Pewter and aluminium do not change colour when heated and they melt at a low temperature, therefore heating is not recommended. Stainless steel, copper and brass shims and foils, woven cloths and wire mesh all react with interesting and varied results. The following experiments show the effect of different heat sources and duration of heating on a range of different metals.

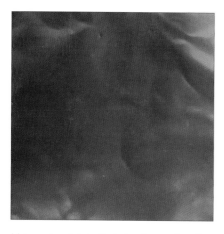 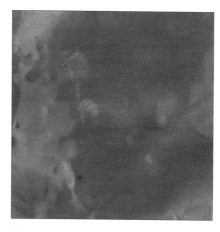 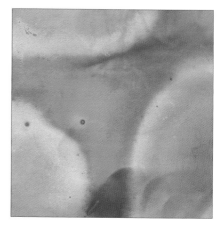

Using a tea light will obviously not give the same heat as a gas cooker. Copper shim was heated over a tea light and two-and-a-half minutes were needed to achieve this all-over rich colour.

After forty-eight seconds this copper shim was showing more colour change when heated over a candle than the tea light achieved in two-and-a-half minutes.

The effect of the gas cooker heat was more dramatic and after twelve seconds this copper shim was showing a number of different colours.

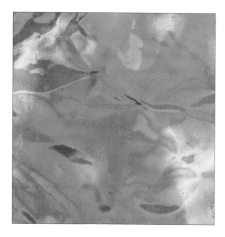 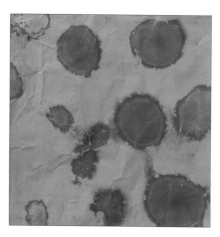 

After twenty-five seconds, copper shim heated with a blow torch showed patches of colour on the areas where the blow torch was directed.

A tea light achieved spots of dark colour on matt copper foil after one minute.

Thick stainless steel mesh (the type used in coffee filter jugs) was heated over a gas cooker for ten seconds.

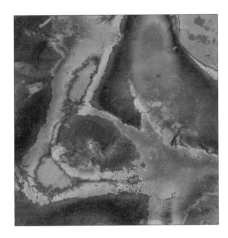

A blow torch directed on to matt copper foil for ten seconds achieved a riot of colour.

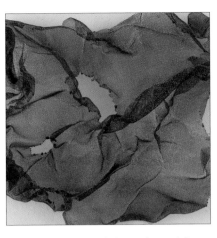

Fine stainless steel cloth was heated for one minute to achieve partial destruction. This can be used when a very distressed surface is required, for example to resemble broken rocks.

Brass wire mesh heated over a candle showed only a darkened area after two minutes.

Seventeen seconds over a gas cooker resulted in this brass wire mesh changing to a blue-grey colour.

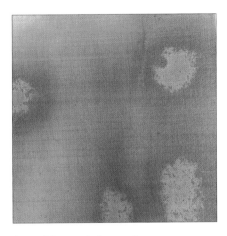

A tea light needed two minutes to change the colour of this copper wire mesh, which showed spotting where the heat was concentrated.

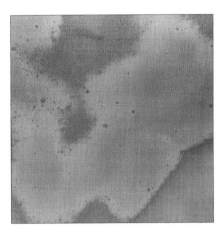

Forty-seven seconds over a candle showed quite a change of colour on this copper wire mesh.

After twenty seconds over the gas cooker, all the natural colour was removed from this copper wire mesh (except where the tongs held the metal).

Fine woven copper cloth was heated with a heat gun for fourteen seconds to achieve this delicate colouring.

Crumpled stainless steel woven cloth was delicately coloured when held over a candle for seven seconds.

Using corrosive substances

It is advisable to use protective gloves when using corrosive substances such as bleach, ammonia, vinegar, lemon juice, salt and patina antiquing agents. Some of these substances will not damage the skin but the hands will be kept clean. Ensure that your work surfaces are well covered with a plastic sheet and newspapers.

A small piece of metal can be treated by putting it in a plastic food bag, adding enough of the corrosive liquid to half cover it and then leaving it to react for a few days or even weeks. The longer the metal is left in the bag, the greater the corrosion. For larger pieces of metal, plastic food trays or a plastic cat litter tray can be used. A respirator mask should always be used when treating metal with ammonia, strong bleaches and patina antiquing agents – do not inhale the fumes.

In the following demonstration, the metal was heat-treated before a corrosive liquid, in this case balsamic vinegar, was applied.

1. Place the metal in a transparent plastic food bag and drizzle in the balsamic vinegar to partially cover the metal.

2. Crease the bag to create folds, so that some parts of the metal are not touching the balsamic vinegar. Leave for two or three days, remove the metal from the bag, rinse in water and pat slightly dry. Further colour change will continue as the sample dries in the air.

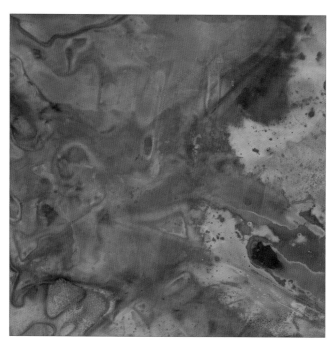

The finished piece shows lines where the metal was not touching the balsamic vinegar in the plastic bag.

On the piece shown opposite, the rectangles display the range of effects that can be achieved with various treatments on different metals. A piece of painted Bondaweb (fusible adhesive mesh) was applied to the background of heat-treated copper wire mesh. All the rectangles were placed on to Aquabond and a sheet of plain, water-soluble film was placed on top, making a sandwich with the rectangles in the middle. This gave a firm pad on which to machine stitch vertical and horizontal lines using a variegated metallic machine embroidery thread between and through the edges of the rectangles. The whole piece was carefully pinned on to a sheet of polystyrene foam to keep it stable before dissolving the soluble film in cold water.

Each of the samples below were first treated for two days with balsamic vinegar, following the method shown on page 34, and then heated over a gas cooker for twelve seconds.

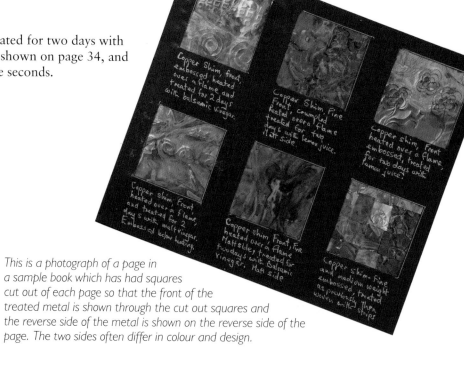

Matt copper foil.

This is a photograph of a page in a sample book which has had squares cut out of each page so that the front of the treated metal is shown through the cut out squares and the reverse side of the metal is shown on the reverse side of the page. The two sides often differ in colour and design.

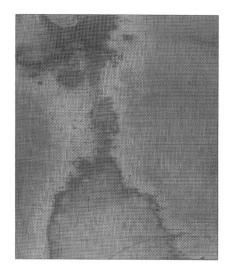

Polished copper foil (the crease lines are quite clear).

Fine copper foil.

Fine woven copper cloth.

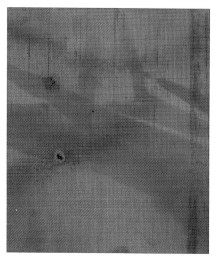

Copper wire mesh.

Brass wire mesh.

Crumpled copper foil.

These samples were heated and then treated with various corrosive substances using the method shown on page 34.

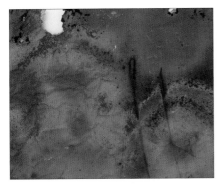

Matt copper foil was soaked in bleach for two days. Notice the erosion of the metal on the top edge. The surface can become quite powdery and encrusted if left longer than two days.

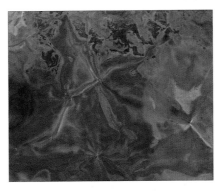

A very rich colour was achieved when matt copper shim was soaked in bleach for two days.

After two days, lemon juice produced a brown and green colour on embossed matt copper foil. An encrusted surface may also be obtained in this short time.

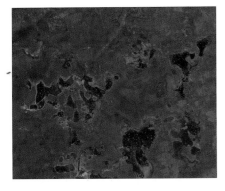

A teaspoonful of salt was sprinkled on to matt copper foil in a plastic bag and left for two days. The resulting colour was a very dark brown and dark green. More than a teaspoonful of salt, left for a week, will achieve greater colour change and some corrosion.

Matt copper foil was treated with balsamic vinegar for two days. Rich dark green patches appeared on a reddish brown background.

Embossed copper shim was treated with lemon juice for two days. The surface is showing the beginning of green encrustations which would increase if the metal were left longer in the lemon juice.

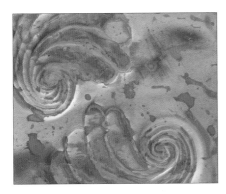

Embossed copper shim was painted with rust activator to produce verdigris. It was left for two days, rinsed with cold water and left to dry. The extent of the verdigris increased whilst drying in the air.

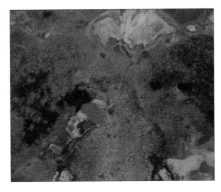

Copper shim was treated with a black patina antiquing agent followed by a rust activator and left for two days. Rich dark colours developed during drying.

Matt copper shim was treated with bleach in a plastic bag and then a day later salt was sprinkled on and it was left for a further two days. Areas were covered in small black crystals and the metal had a wonderful crusty surface when dry.

Adding texture

Texture can be added by drawing on metal by hand using an old, empty biro or an embossing tool; by running a pastry wheel or a pinwheel over the surface; by passing it through a ribbler (crimper); or by stamping it with a commercial stamp machine. All these utensils create very different textures. Using an embossing tool or biro enables you to draw your own design or to go over a previously traced design. Lines can be drawn with a pastry wheel or a pinwheel and deep ridges can be achieved by using a ribbler (crimper). Ribblers are available with varying patterns, as shown on page 40. Depending on the source of the metal, heating before embossing on copper can sometimes increase the ease with which the embossing tool moves.

Key

Based on a traditional tapa design, this pattern was embossed by hand on to heavy-weight copper shim. The metal was then painted with black acrylic paint which was quickly wiped off leaving only a suggestion of colour. Purple and green polish was applied by hand, then gold polish was applied to the raised surfaces.

Copper foil was first embossed then painted with black acrylic paint, as in the example above. The paint was wiped off leaving very little colour then various coloured polishes were lightly applied by hand. A final layer of thinly applied black acrylic paint was applied and wiped off producing a speckled surface where it touched the polish.

Heat-treated copper shim was decorated by running a pinwheel and a pastry wheel over the surface.

Embossing

When embossing metal with an embossing tool, you will need a pad on which to place the metal. This can be a pad of newspaper, a craft cutting mat or a computer mouse mat. Using the embossing tool, press down firmly on to the back of the metal, taking care not to press too firmly or the metal will be punctured. If a deep ridge is required, turn the metal over to the right side and emphasise the ridge by running a blunt wooden embossing tool down either side of it. Potters' and model-makers' tools can be useful when embossing metal, as can different kitchen utensils, for example cheese graters and pastry cutters. The metal can be embossed before or after heating and then paint, polish, inks or dyes can be used for colouring.

1. Draw the design on the back of the untreated copper shim with a biro.

2. Draw over the pattern again with a thicker embossing tool to deepen the indentations.

3. The embossed image is shown on the front/right side of the copper and is now ready to be heat-treated and decorated.

A rectangle of heat-treated copper shim was embossed with a design taken from the tapa cloths of the Pacific (drawn first in my sketchbook, shown below). Black acrylic paint was brushed on and partially wiped off. I then used my finger to rub on maroon, green and black polish, and black acrylic paint was applied again and quickly wiped off. Finally, I rubbed gold polish over the raised embossed pattern, again using my finger.

I keep a sketchbook in which to record my design ideas.

Use a pastry wheel (left) and a pinwheel (right) to create texture by running the wheels firmly over the surface of the metal (not too firmly or you will puncture the metal).

Ribblers (crimpers) are available with various designs embossed on the two rollers. Simply feed the metal in through the rollers on one side, twist the handle and the embossed version will emerge from the other side.

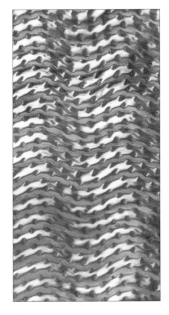

Heat-treated copper shim, ribbled vertically then horizontally.

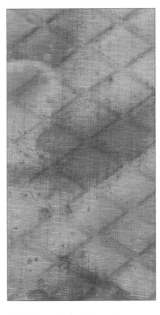

Heat-treated copper wire mesh embossed with a diamond-patterned ribbler.

Heat-treated copper wire mesh with ribbled horizontal lines.

Heat-treated matt copper foil, stamped with an Indian printing block then put through the diamond ribbler.

Brass wire mesh ribbled with a diamond pattern.

Heat-treated brass wire mesh showing ribbled horizontal lines.

Heat-treated matt copper foil ribbled vertically and horizontally.

Heat-treated brass foil, ribbled with a diamond pattern, then randomly painted within the diamonds with glass paints.

42

The 'decaying floor of a bogwood' is the theme for this piece of work. The 'floor' was built up using layers of black felt, velvet, painted Bondaweb (fusible adhesive mesh) and a piece of stamped wire mesh. Oak leaves of copper shim were embossed and stitched in place on the background. Two layers of black chiffon were stitched randomly over the surface and distressed with a craft heat gun before walnut ink was used to darken the 'decaying' surface.

The sample on the left illustrates some of the methods used when embossing. Going anticlockwise, from top left: hand embossing on heat-treated copper shim using a biro; texture created by hand embossing using a fine embossing tool; heat-treated brass wire mesh embossed diagonally with a pastry wheel; heat-treated copper shim embossed with a pastry wheel diagonally in two directions; heat-treated copper shim hand embossed with an embossing tool; aluminium embossed with a commercial stamp machine.

Adding colour

Paints, dyes and inks can be applied to metal by various methods. The most common methods of application are by paintbrush, stencil brush, sponge brush, nail varnish brush, printing block, spray can or even your finger.

For colouring large areas of metal a paint or print roller can be used, even over scrunched, creased or embossed metal. Alternatively, the roller can be covered with paint, rolled over a printing block and the painted printing block then placed face down on the metal. For small printing blocks paint can be applied with a cotton bud (see page 49) or sponge brush.

On the panel shown opposite (and on page 29), each square of heat-treated copper shim was hand embossed with the same design and brushed with black acrylic paint which was quickly wiped off with absorbent paper. A number of different types of paints, glass paints, nail varnishes, polishes and glue with foiling were applied as listed below. The petals of the flowers were painted with colours chosen not only to blend together but also to show the variety of applications. Once painted, each of these copper shim squares was stitched on to a slightly larger square of heat-treated copper wire mesh, and finally all the squares were applied to a black felt background.

Key

Bronze metallic paint was applied thickly with a small paintbrush.

Purple paint gel was applied using the nozzle on the bottle.

Orange glass paint was applied with a small paintbrush.

Purple polish was applied with a cotton bud.

Thick, green-gold ink was applied with a paintbrush.

Glitter was sprinkled on to wet metallic paint.

Black puff paint was heated and gold polish was rubbed with a finger on the raised areas.

Glue applied to the flower was foiled in purple.

Blue polish was applied with a small paintbrush.

A cotton bud was used to apply glue before covering with an embossing powder.

Shiny purple nail varnish appears very dark on this sample.

A slightly dull, matt, dark green glass paint was applied by paintbrush.

Materials for adding colour

As we have seen in the preceding sections, the initial steps to creating colour and pattern on metal are to heat it and then to use chemicals to further alter its colour and appearance.

Adding paints, dyes, inks, nail varnish, polishes, etc. will make these changes even more dramatic. Painting embossed, heat-treated copper with black acrylic paint, for example, and then wiping off the surplus will produce an antiqued look, which can then be further coloured with polishes applied by finger or by brush.

Water-based paints are not usually successful as they do not adhere to the polished surface, but they will perform quite well if painted on to the heat-treated matt side of copper foil. In my experience, metallic paint is usually the most effective paint. Alcohol-based inks or spirit dyes add an intensely bright colour, and when two or more colours are dropped from the nozzle of the bottle, they merge into each other to create a richly coloured glaze.

Painting a printing block with metallic paint, PVA glue or puff paint (dimensional paint) and placing the

block on the metal is another decorative way of adding colour. A red shimmer leafing pen can cover metal in small areas and is easy to use in the grooves created by embossing. For bold colours, nail varnish and glass paints are easily applied.

When cleaning brushes, cotton buds or sponges, remember to clean them in water when using water-based paints and inks, or a solvent if they are spirit-based. Allow any paint, particularly black acrylic, to partially dry and then wipe off the excess to give a slightly distressed look and a surface to further decorate

with other colouring agents. Spirit-soluble dyes (wood dyes) react with methylated spirits to produce interesting results.

Embossing powders or glitter sprinkled on to wet paints or gels can give a sparkling effect, but be sure to check that they will accept heat before using a heat gun on the embossing powders.

Always experiment, but take care to read the precautions on the bottle you are using; wear protective gloves and a respirator mask where necessary; and protect your work surfaces.

Stencilling

One of the most effective mediums for stencilling on to metal is metallic paint, applied using a sponge brush to produce a mottled effect. If you want to try watercolour paints, dyes or inks, a wash of black acrylic paint applied first to the copper or brass and then quickly wiped off gives a surface which is more receptive to stencilling with these alternatives. It is always advisable to experiment with any paint or ink on a small piece of metal before committing yourself to using a large piece for a project.

1. Place the stencil over the metal and position it carefully. If it is a large stencil, secure it to the surface you are working on with masking tape.

2. Hold the stencil firmly in place and apply the paint with a sponge brush. Press down gently, covering all the holes in the stencil. The sponge gives the paint a mottled effect. Alternatively, a stencil brush can be used.

3. Carefully lift off the stencil to reveal the design underneath.

Using masking tape or glue as a resist

The same techniques for colouring copper and brass as mentioned above can be used when using either masking tape or PVA glue. Embossed, ribbled or plain metal can also produce some good results.

In this example, narrow strips of masking tape have been used to cover areas which are to remain free of paint. Paint has then been applied to the whole area and, when dry, the tape has been removed to reveal the metal beneath.

The flower shapes shown above were drawn on the metal using PVA glue applied through the nozzle of the glue bottle. When the glue was dry, spirit dyes were painted over the whole piece. Spirit dye dries quickly and the glue flower was then peeled off to reveal the bare metal underneath.

This design was created by applying uneven spots of PVA glue in a random pattern on to crumpled metal before it was painted. The spots of glue were then removed.

Freehand painting

The application of paint to metal usually follows heat treatment and embossing, and can be before or after stitching. If the purpose of the stitching is to create texture but not to add colour, then the stitching can be painted over. Always protect your work surface with newspaper and place the metal on a piece of absorbent paper before painting. Wear protective gloves when using spirit dyes, paints or inks to avoid staining your fingers.

1. For a small piece of metal such as this piece of pewter, load a cotton bud with spirit dye and spread the colour over the surface. For a larger piece of metal the spirit dye can be dropped from the nozzle of the bottle and allowed to spread by tilting the metal from side to side.

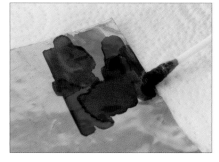

2. Apply further colours in the same way, allowing them to merge naturally on the metal surface. The metal can be moved as suggested above to allow the different colours to flow into each other. The colour can also be applied with a sponge brush or a small paintbrush.

This piece of heat-treated matt copper foil was put through a ribbler (crimper) creating a diamond pattern. Some of the diamonds were painted with nail varnish using a nail varnish brush, others using a fine painting brush; the edges of the former were found not to be as clearly defined as the latter.

This piece of copper shim was textured with a ribbler in both directions then coloured with a spirit dye using a paintbrush.

Copper shim was embossed using an empty biro, then painted with two different coloured spirit dyes that were merged together with a paintbrush. Gold polish was rubbed with a finger on the raised surface.

The same technique was used as in the previous sample but the metal used was part of a tomato purée tube.

Colouring an embossed image

Embossed metal can be painted but also coloured using a polish. With only a hint of one or more colours your work assumes a greater depth when the embossed design is highlighted with a gold polish, as shown below.

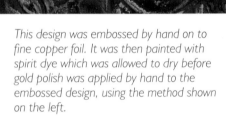

1. Pick up the polish by gently stroking the colour with the pad of your finger, making sure the fingernail does not pick up a small wedge of polish. Choose the finger with the greatest pad (or shortest nail).

2. Gently stroke the colour on to the embossed surface so that it adheres only to the raised parts, leaving bare metal in the indents. In this sample, the side being coloured is the side on which the metal was embossed, which is usually referred to as the reverse side. The main body of the metal is raised and therefore coloured, and in the indented lines and pouncing (see page 68) the metal remains bare.

This design was embossed by hand on to fine copper foil. It was then painted with spirit dye which was allowed to dry before gold polish was applied by hand to the embossed design, using the method shown on the left.

A strip of quite heavy copper shim was pressed over a biscuit cutter, with the metal pressed firmly over the sides of the cutter to give a pronounced embossing effect. The metal was turned over and the same process repeated on the other side in different areas, producing a design that was both raised and indented on each side. A purple metallic paint was brushed over the surface, with silver and black polishes enhancing the design.

A traced design was embossed on to crumpled, heat-treated copper foil. Black acrylic paint was brushed on and quickly wiped off. Walnut wood dye was then brushed over and, when dry, green, red and gold polishes were rubbed over the surface with a finger.

A background of black felt gives a firm base on to which patches of varying sizes are woven and applied (see page 94). The metals used are heat-treated copper shim; matt and polished copper foils; and wire mesh. Various designs were embossed on the metals, which were painted, sprayed with webbing spray or highlighted with polish, and then woven. Braids of stitched and painted Vilene (craft interfacing) were wound with wrapped (stitched) wires and added to the weaving process. By using different widths and lengths for the patches the panel initially does not appear to be woven.

Printing

Printing with Indian blocks or plastic blocks is a decorative way of transferring paint and designs to metal. Acrylic and metallic paints are very effective but always experiment to see if the block will hold the dye or ink you have chosen. PVA glue, foiling glue and Xpandaprint (puff paint) produce a raised surface which can be polished, foiled or, in the case of PVA glue, used as a resist which is then peeled off later. For a large printing block, a layer of paint can be applied using a roller. Place the paint on a small, flat surface, roll the roller over it to collect the paint, then roll it over the printing block.

Printing with metallic paint

1. Apply the paint carefully to the design on the printing block using a cotton bud.

2. Press the coloured block firmly on to the metal.

3. Carefully lift off the block, revealing the image transferred to the metal underneath. If the design is only partially printed do not worry as this can create a more interesting effect than if the whole image is visible.

Printing with PVA glue and Xpandaprint (puff paint)

The pieces of heat-treated metal shown on this page have been decorated using the same Indian printing block as that used on the previous page.

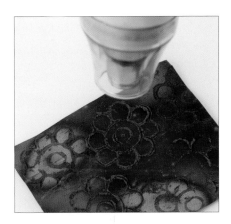

The flowers with the raised, dark outlines were printed using Xpandaprint; the others were printed with PVA glue.

A heat gun was directed for a few minutes on to the flowers printed with the Xpandaprint until it began to bubble.

The raised outlines of the other flowers created using PVA glue were coloured using gold polish applied with a finger.

A greater amount of puff paint was applied to heat-treated copper foil to raise the outline even more. The whole piece was painted with walnut spirit dye and then, when dry, gold polish was rubbed with a finger over the raised design.

53

A printing block with a large leaf design was applied to heat-treated matt copper foil using bronze metallic paint.

A background of heat-treated matt copper foil was used to display this Indian printing block design in blue metallic paint.

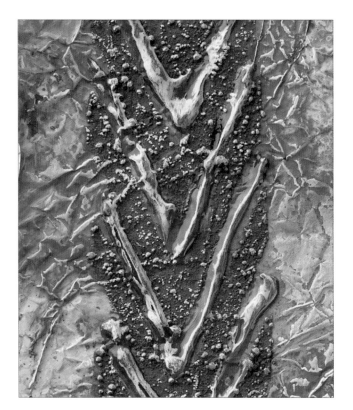

A printing block with a 'V' design was covered with black Xpandaprint (puff paint) and printed on to creased, heat-treated matt copper foil, then heated using a heat gun to raise the surface. PVA glue was piped on to the metal from the nozzle of the bottle, into the spaces between the Xpandaprint 'V' designs. Gold polish was rubbed on to the raised surfaces of the creased metal, the puff paint and the PVA glue.

This panel illustrates the use of an Indian printing block in four different ways: 1. heat-treated copper shim was pressed over the block by hand and the lines emphasised with an embossing pen (shown upper left); 2. a mould of the block was made using water-soluble paper, the edges of which were merged on to the metal when damp (shown below it to the right); 3. a piece of Lutradur was printed with the design, stitched, heat-treated and then stitched on to the metal (top right); 4. the block design was printed directly on to the metal background areas not previously treated. The finished panel was covered with black chiffon, free machine stitched around the designs and distressed with a heat gun.

Foiling

Two methods of foiling are shown here: using powdered glue (as used in dress-making) and using foiling glue applied from the nozzle of the bottle. The lines of foiling glue on the heat-treated copper shim shown below are a simple way to demonstrate how easy it is to foil. Powdered glue gives a very different result, as can be seen on page 57. Never throw away a sheet of used foil as it can always be used again.

Foiling using foiling glue

1. Apply the glue supplied with the foiling sheet, controlling it to create the design you require.

2. Leave the glue to dry until it becomes clear. It will then be ready to foil.

3. Lay the foil, colour side up, over the top of the design and rub the foil firmly where the glue has been placed. If you want to add more than one colour, leave some of the design bare. You can lift the foil to check you have covered the glue where required.

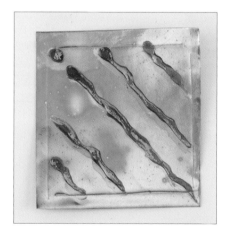

4. Lift off the sheet of foil, revealing the coloured design underneath.

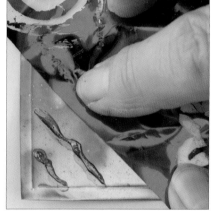

5. Apply a second colour following the same method, focusing on the bare areas of the glue.

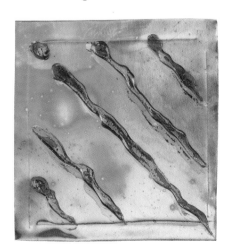

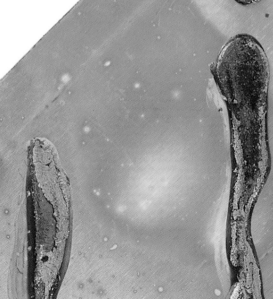

The completed design.

Foiling using powdered glue

1. Lay the piece of metal on a sheet of parchment and sprinkle the glue on to the metal.

2. Lay a sheet of foil over the top, coloured side up.

3. Lay a second sheet of parchment over the foil and press it firmly with a warm iron. This causes the foil to adhere to the powdered glue. Ensure that the powdered glue does not fall on to the ironing board cover and that the iron does not come in contact with the glue.

4. Remove the parchment and the foil to reveal the design underneath. As mentioned on page 56, always save the used foil sheet because only a little foil is removed each time.

To create this design, glue was painted on to Indian printing blocks which were then stamped on to a piece of heat-treated matt copper metal foil. Foil was applied in the same way as above.

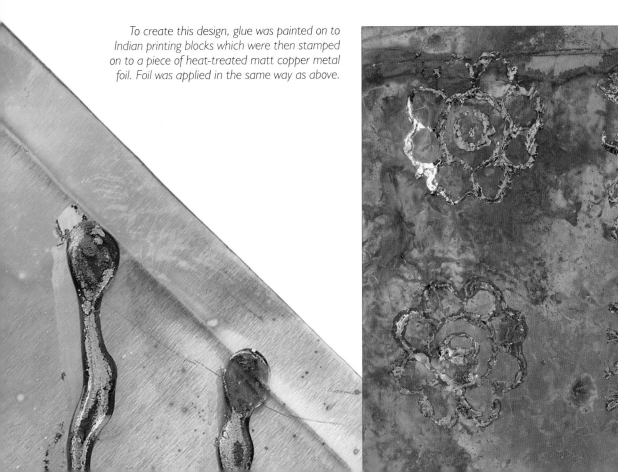

Adding embossing powder and glitter

Embossing powder and glitter can be sprinkled on to glue, paint or nail varnish. When heat is applied to the embossing powder the surface will change. Glue applied to a printing block can be stamped on to the metal, embossing powder sprinkled on and then heat applied. Always check that the paint, ink or glue you use will accept heat if the embossing powder is to be heated to set.

The design shown here was stamped on to the metal with glue and then covered with embossing powder.

1. Paint nail varnish on the metal in the areas you wish to colour.

2. Sprinkle on the embossing powder.

3. Tip the excess embossing powder back into the pot. The embossing powder can be left unheated or, if glue has been used, heated to produce a different effect.

This piece of heat-treated copper shim has been cut out with decorative-edged craft scissors. A pastry wheel and a pinwheel have created an uneven grid of marks. Different coloured nail varnishes have been painted on to some of the rectangles and glitter or embossing powder was sprinkled on before the nail varnish was dry.

Webbing spray

Cans containing webbing spray have to be shaken for a long time to achieve success (this is always specified on the tin). The can is held at an angle and moved from left to right over the metal with quite a fast movement. The spray falls out of the can as a web and floats down on to the metal; a thicker web can be made by a repeat or slower movement. This should be done in the open air as the fumes are quite strong. Use a protective layer of newspapers to protect the lawn or path.

This effect was achieved by spraying gold-coloured webbing spray on to heat-treated matt copper foil.

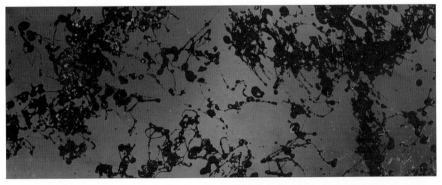

This sample shows heat-treated copper foil sprayed quite slowly with black webbing spray resulting in a thick web in some places.

Heat-treated copper wire mesh was sprayed with gold-coloured webbing spray, showing different thicknesses of webbing.

Copper shim was heat-treated, sprayed first with black and then with a fine, gold-coloured webbing spray.

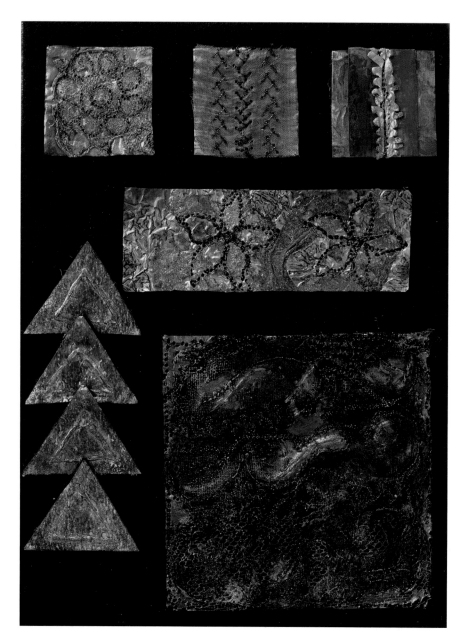

The design on this sample was embossed by hand on to heat-treated copper shim. Black acrylic paint was applied and partially wiped off and a purple spirit dye was then added. Once dry, I used my finger to apply green and purple polishes over the surface, and finally to rub gold polish over the raised surface of the embossing. The metal was stitched on to black felt using free machine stitching around the edge of the design. The felt was then cut out around the edge of the stitching.

This panel shows examples of various techniques. The two outer squares at the top show the use of decorative surface finishes, which were heat-treated. The middle square is of ribbled copper shim with a metallic gauze fabric applied with a decorative automatic machine stitch.

The triangles are copper shim, treated with painted Bondaweb (fusible adhesive mesh) and with foiled triangles applied. Black polish has been rubbed with a finger over each triangle. The rectangle of crumpled, heat-treated copper foil has had painted garden fleece stitched on in a flower design, which was then heat distressed.

The large square of heat-treated embossed copper shim shows partially wiped-off black acrylic paint with layers of net, vanishing muslin and black chiffon secured with stitching beside the embossed lines. A heat gun was used to partially disintegrate the layers.

On the panel shown opposite, a black felt background is just visible between the patches, which have been treated using different techniques. Embossing, block printing with glass paint, glue and Xpandaprint (puff paint) are just some of the techniques shown. All methods used are explained in the preceding sections of this book.

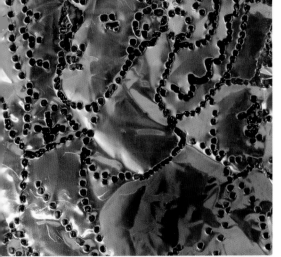

Stitching

The techniques for machine stitching on metal are the same as those for stitching on fabrics. The first step is to start with straight stitching. Place the piece of metal on to a backing of Vilene (craft interfacing), use a sewing machine needle size 90/14 and a machine thread of your choice, and begin to stitch (see page 64). Straight stitch, zig-zag stitch and decorative automatic machine stitches all require the presser foot to be on and the feed dog up. Free machine stitching requires the presser foot to be replaced with an open toe or darning foot and the feed dog to be dropped. With some sewing machines the feed dog cannot be dropped but there is a metal plate available to cover it.

Free machine stitching can be used in many ways. For example, it can emphasise a design when used to outline a stamped printing block image as seen on page 55. Alternatively, filling the stamped image with free machine stitching and then painting over it gives a textured effect to the same design. When free machine stitching on pewter to achieve a filigree silver effect, a size 100/16 machine needle can be used. Zig-zag stitch can also be used when free machine stitching, which gives a very different effect from stitching with the feed dog up and the presser foot on.

Fine fabrics can be stitched on to metal and then either partially cut away to reveal some of the metal or left in place to allow only a glimpse of metal showing through. Used with Angelina fibres, chiffon and organza over a metal background, free machine stitching unites all the materials to give an attractive background on which to place other stitched items. A quick blast from a heat gun further integrates the materials if a distressed image is required. When free machine stitching a material such as Lutradur on to a metal background and distressing it with a heat gun, dense stitching leaves only a small area of Lutradur to disintegrate; less stitching achieves more disintegration. However, it is also possible to hand stitch on metal, although the same results will not be achieved as those when machine stitching. It is worth experimenting to see what new techniques can be discovered.

Decorative automatic machine stitches can be used on metals but it is advisable to choose patterns with stitches not too close together otherwise there will be a tendency for the stitches to pile up on each other and create a large hole.

Wire can be decorated by zig-zag free machine stitching over it (see page 117). Beaded wire can also be treated in the same way but make sure you guide the beads to avoid the needle when zig-zag stitching over it. Cords can be made in this way using several decorative threads twisted together and then free machine stitched with a zig-zag stitch (see page 116).

Sewing machines should always be cleaned regularly to remove fluff and threads, and always clean the machine after using metal. Decorative surface finishes and minute slivers of metal, paint and other substances can occasionally drop under the feed dog. This is unlikely but there will be no problems if the machine is cleaned frequently.

Casket

length x width x height: 23.5 x 11.5 x 22cm (9¼ x 4½ x 8¾in)

This casket was based on the Thomas Becket casket exhibited at the Victoria and Albert Museum, London. Stitched panels of copper shim were attached to a background of dyed Vilene (craft interfacing), together with dyed hessian, muslin and chiffon. The copper panels were heat-treated after stitching to give a distressed and antiqued appearance. Various cords and braids were added for decoration and edgings. The silver metallic silk lining was stitched with a decorative automatic machine stitch. One side of the lid opens to give access to the casket.

Starting to stitch

Set up your sewing machine for straight stitching with the feed dog up and the standard presser foot on. Use a size 100/16 needle and put silver metallic thread on the spool and in the bobbin. The spool tension should be set on Auto or Normal. A slightly larger piece of backing fabric than the piece of metal should be used to allow for the slight movement of the metal when stitching, as shown in steps 1, 2 and 3 below.

1. Select a suitable backing fabric such as bump and take a slightly smaller piece of pewter. The excess bump can be trimmed off after stitching is finished.

2. Thread your machine with silver metallic thread, place the metal on top of the bump backing and put the two layers under the needle. Lower the presser foot.

3. Initially holding the two threads, start to stitch in the usual way, after ensuring the feed dog is up and the presser foot down.

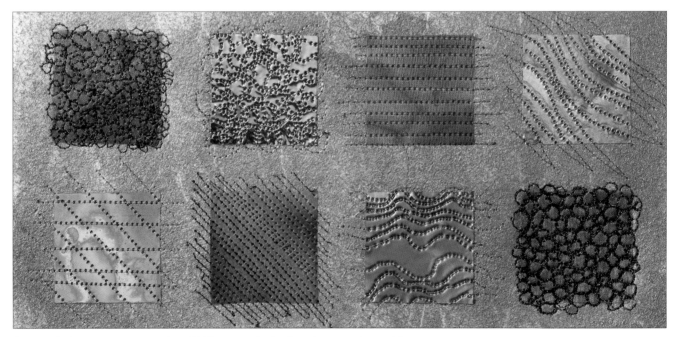

The panel above provides examples of different methods of stitching metal on to Vilene, which has been previously painted with metallic paint. It is also an excellent way of experimenting with different ways of stitching on various metals and proving to yourself how easy it really is.

Brooch

This stylish brooch is simple to make and provides an excellent introduction to straight stitching on metal. It measures approximately 3.5 x 5cm (1½ x 2in) but you can adapt the instructions and the materials required to make any size brooch you wish.

Materials

Copper shim, 4.5 x 6.5cm (1¾ x 2½in) (allow more than the finished size of the brooch)

Black felt, minimum 3.5 x 5cm (1½ x 2in)

Red felt, approximately 5.5 x 7.5cm (2¼ x 3in) (this quantity allows for any movement of the copper when stitching)

Green wire, machine-wrapped with green and black variegated machine embroidery thread, 61cm (24in)

Copper metallic machine embroidery thread

Glass paints and paintbrush

All-purpose glue

Scissors for cutting metal

Fabric scissors

Commercial brooch fastening

1. Machine stitch the copper shim to the red felt backing using straight stitch. Begin by working evenly spaced lines, approximately 0.5cm (¼in) apart, down the length of the metal, then work the rows horizontally creating squares. Either judge the spacing by the help of your sewing machine or measure and mark out the columns and rows before you start.

2. Trim around the outside along the stitching lines, leaving a rectangle six squares wide and eight deep (approximately 3.5 x 5cm, or 1½ x 2in).

3. Paint some of the squares using glass paints in your own choice of colours and put to one side to dry.

4. Wrap a length of the machine-wrapped wire (see page 117) around the brooch following alternate stitching lines, twisting the two ends together at the back to secure.

5. Cut a piece of black felt to the exact size of the brooch. Apply a strong all-purpose glue to the back of the brooch and attach it to the black felt lining.

6. Attach the brooch pin to the back of the brooch.

The finished brooch.

Free machining

When free machining, the feed dog is dropped. If, though, this method is not possible with your machine, a special plate can be used to cover it. The work can now be moved freely once the presser foot has been replaced with an open toe or darning foot. To achieve the best results, use an average speed with smooth, even movements. Being aware of possible problems will help to avoid them. A size 100/16 needle has been used to stitch the samples of pewter on page 67, and a size 90/14 for the copper samples shown below. If the metal starts to flake in a small area, a thin layer of PVA glue can be applied to hold the metal flakes in place.

A backing fabric such as bump or felt should be used to enable the sharp edges of the metal to bed down into it. This also prevents the bed of the sewing machine from getting scratched. Wire mesh does not usually require a backing fabric.

Free machining has been used to create texture within a printed and embossed design on heat-treated copper shim.

Use free machining to create a design in thread, such as this one using copper metallic thread on heat-treated copper wire mesh.

PVA glue has been applied in a thin line to heat-treated matt copper foil, and free machining has been used to follow the lines of the glue and the design created by heat treatment.

In this example, a rapid speed and a slow movement of the metal under the needle have resulted in numerous overlapping holes that give a rough appearance to the surface of the metal. However, there may be occasions when this type of finish is required, so it is worth remembering how to achieve it.

A slower speed and smooth, controlled movements have resulted in a more even pattern of stitching, which is required when aiming for a surface resembling filigree silver.

The cover of this needlecase is made of free machine stitched pewter using silver metallic machine embroidery thread. It is backed with purple felt and inside it has two double pieces of white felt secured down the spine in which to place the needles.

Pendant

This striking pendant is easy to make and is a good demonstration of the use of free machining. It measures 5.5cm (2¼in) in diameter but this can be adjusted to any size you wish.

Materials

Two pieces of pewter, 7 x 7cm (2¾ x 2¾in)

Bump for backing fabric and padding, approximately 23 x 18cm (9 x 7in)

Silver ring, 6 or 7mm (approximately ¼in)

Silver chain or black leather cord with silver fastening

Silver metallic machine embroidery thread

Silver and black variegated machine embroidery thread

50cm (19¾in) silver cord made from three lengths of silver threads stitched together using black and silver variegated machine embroidery thread (see page 116)

Embossing tool

Scissors for cutting metal

Fabric scissors

1. Cut two pewter circles, 5.5cm (2¼in) in diameter and place one of them on a piece of bump slightly larger than the pewter. Free machine stitch over the pewter using the silver metallic thread and a 100/16 needle, leaving your design unstitched in the centre.

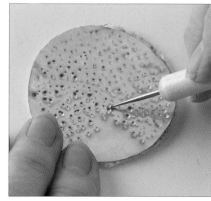

2. Cut a piece of bump the same size as the pewter circles. Lay the second piece of pewter over the top of it and cover the pewter in a random pattern of indentations using an embossing tool. This is known as pouncing and will form a smooth back for the pendant.

3. Trim off the excess bump around the edge of the first circle of pewter. Thread a silver ring on to the hand-made cord and attach the cord to the pewter by stitching around it using a zig-zag machine stitch and the silver and black thread. Fold the ends of the cords under the pewter and bump on starting and finishing to make a neat join. Ensure the ring is positioned at the top of the pendant. Stitch the cord around the other piece of pewter (the back of the pendant) in the same way.

4. Make the padding for the pendant to give a raised centre. Cut out ten circular pieces of bump in five different sizes (two of each size); the largest should be just slightly smaller than the pendant. Place them in two piles with the largest pieces at the bottom. Spray between the layers with temporary adhesive spray.

5. Sandwich the two piles between the two pewter circles, with the smallest pieces of bump touching in the centre. Overstitch by hand using the silver and black thread, placing just a few stitches around the outside of the pendant to hold the padding in place, before stitching on the sewing machine using a zig-zag stitch.

6. Using your sewing machine, zig-zag stitch the two sides of the pendant together using the silver and black thread, carefully stitching either side of the silver ring.

This photograph shows a variety of pendants made using the technique shown on page 68.
The square-shaped pendant has a flower attached to the front piece of stitched pewter
before stitching the front and back pieces together. (See pages 70 to 71 for details for
making the flower.)

Oval pewter box

This easily made oval pewter lidded box has been created using the type of inexpensive plain cardboard box found in craft shops. Silver ink has been used to paint the inside and the outside of the box but not the top of the lid.

Materials

Two pieces of pewter, one 7 x 5cm (2¾ x 2in) and one 4.5 x 4.5cm (1¾ x 1¾in) for the flower

Bump, 8 x 6cm (3¼ x 2¼in)

Blank oval cardboard box with lid, 5 x 6.5cm (2 x 2½in), painted inside and out (except for the top of the lid) using silver ink

Three small beads

Silver metallic machine embroidery thread

20cm (7¾in) of cord made from three lengths of silver thread stitched together using black and silver sewing thread (see page 116)

Strong all-purpose glue

Shot silk, 4.5 x 4.5cm (1¾ x 1¾in)

Scissors for cutting metal

Fabric scissors

Biro

Embossing tool

Sewing needle

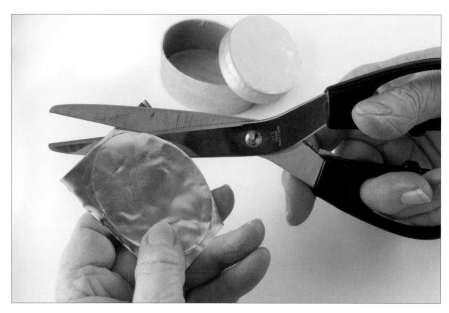

1. Cut out a piece of pewter the same size as the lid of the box. The simplest way to do this is to draw with a biro around the lid straight on to the pewter. You should cut slightly inside the drawn outline to allow for the width of the cord, which will be stitched around the edge.

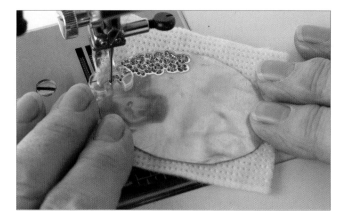

2. Place the pewter on a piece of bump (or other backing fabric) cut slightly larger than the pewter and free machine stitch all over the surface using silver metallic thread, leaving a narrow edge free of stitching around the outside of the pewter.

3. Cut off the excess bump and stitch on the cord using a zig-zag stitch and the same silver thread as before.

4. Draw the flower design on to a piece of pewter using a biro or embossing tool. Place it on a lining of coloured shot silk and machine stitch around the outline using the silver thread. Carefully cut out the flower around the outside of the stitching.

5. Sew three tiny coloured beads in the centre of the flower by hand using two strands of the silver thread.

6. Leave the thread on the needle and use it to attach the flower to the pewter.

7. Glue the pewter to the top of the lid using strong all-purpose glue.

The completed box.

The larger oval pewter box has an initial left unstitched in the centre of the free machining on the lid. On the pewter lid of the smaller circular box, the free machining has been coloured with pink dye.

Rectangular pewter box

Lined with red felt, this rectangular pewter box is the perfect size to store small items of jewellery such as earrings. If the box is much larger, such as the one shown on pages 76 and 77, there will be a need to have an inner lining of balsa wood to support and strengthen the panels of pewter.

This box has been lined with red felt, but you could choose any lining fabric you wish. Please read through the instructions before embarking on this project.

Template

The template provided below is for the red felt and the Vilene. It is reproduced two-thirds actual size and therefore needs to be enlarged by fifty per cent. Use the same template for the pewter panels, but make each panel 1mm (⅟₂₀in) smaller along each side to allow enough room for the cord edging.

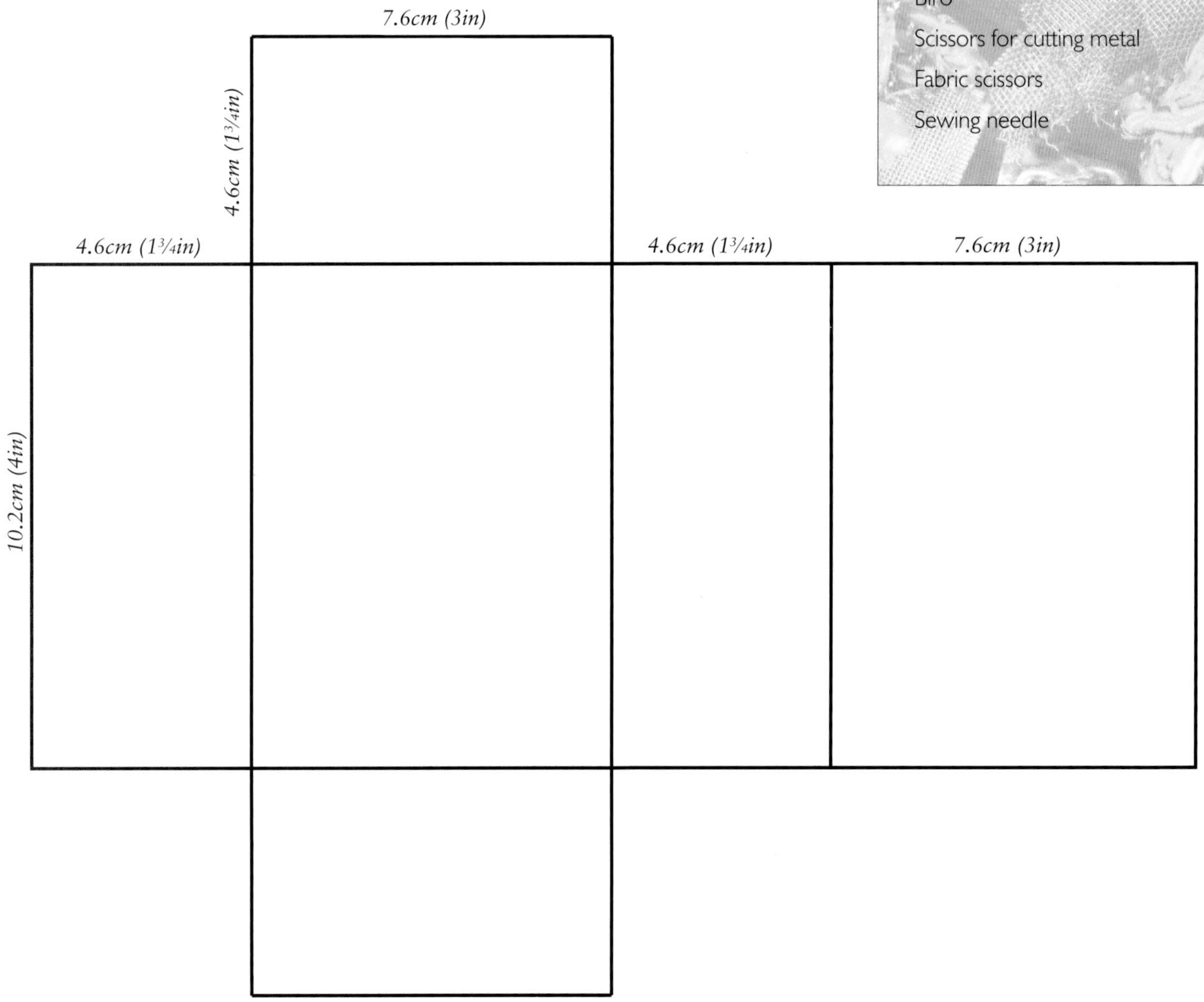

7.6cm (3in)

4.6cm (1¾in)

4.6cm (1¾in)

4.6cm (1¾in)

7.6cm (3in)

10.2cm (4in)

1. Cut out a piece of Vilene (craft interfacing) and a piece of felt using the template provided. Draw lines on the Vilene using a biro and a ruler to mark the edges of the box. Spray the reverse of the Vilene with temporary adhesive spray and place it on top of the felt. This will hold the two fabrics in place to enable you to stitch them together, using the lines drawn on the Vilene. Thread your sewing machine with a variegated metallic machine embroidery thread and use a straight stitch.

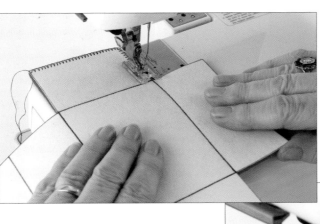

2. Using the same thread, zig-zag stitch around the outside edge of the shape.

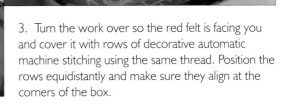

3. Turn the work over so the red felt is facing you and cover it with rows of decorative automatic machine stitching using the same thread. Position the rows equidistantly and make sure they align at the corners of the box.

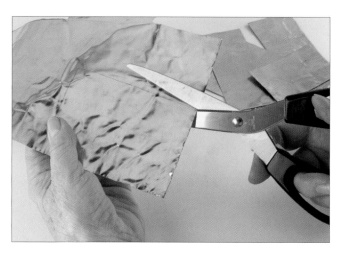

4. Using a zig-zag stitch and the same thread, attach the cord to the outside of the shape.

5. Cut out the individual pewter panels for all the sides of the box. These can be cut from a single piece of pewter. Use the template provided but cut just inside the drawn line to allow for the addition of the cord. Careful planning is needed to fit the pieces into the rectangle; plan their positions before starting to cut.

6. Put the panel for the base of the box to one side. Place each of the other panels on a piece of bump that is slightly larger than the pewter and free machine stitch over the surface of each panel using the silver metallic thread to imitate filigree silver. Do not stitch over the edge of the pewter but leave a 1mm (1/20in) rim around the perimeter. Trim off the excess bump. For the base, cut a piece of bump the same size as the pewter and machine stitch the two layers together around the edge of the panel using a straight stitch and the silver metallic thread. Pounce the pewter as shown on page 68.

7. Attach a length of hand-made cord around the outside of each panel using a zig-zag stitch worked in the variegated metallic thread.

8. Join all the pewter panels together in the shape of the felt template. Tightly push the two sides together where two panels join and zig-zag stitch them together using the variegated metallic thread.

9. Make two flowers using the method described on pages 70 and 71 and attach them to the lid of the box.

10. Make the fastening for the lid by threading a short length of cord and wire through a decorative silver bead and zig-zag stitching the ends of the cord together using silver thread. Strengthen the cord by working up and down several times from the ends to the bead.

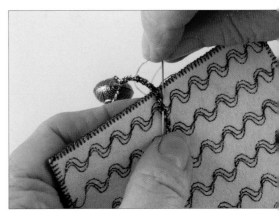

11. Attach the cord and bead to the lining of the box, sewing it on to the Vilene, at the front of the lid. Make sure that the stitching does not show through the felt on the other side.

12. Spray the bump backing of the pewter shape with temporary adhesive and lay the lining, felt uppermost, on top. Oversew the two layers together at each corner with a few hand stitches to hold them in place, then machine stitch around the outside edge of the two double layers using a zig-zag stitch and the variegated metallic thread. You should now have a flat shape with the pewter on one side and the red felt lining on the other.

13. Fold the shape into a box and oversew the corners together by hand using the variegated metallic thread, doubled for extra strength, to hold it in place. When all four corners are secure, oversew the sides together as shown in the photograph, easing the edges together.

The completed box.

75

(Anticlockwise, starting top left): the large oblong box requires an inner lining between the decorative red silk lining of the box and the outer layer of pewter on Vilene. Balsa wood is light in weight but gives rigidity to the length of pewter; the two smaller rectangular pewter boxes are similar to the one on page 75, one of which has been coloured using red dye; the conical lidded box is made using the same technique as the rectangular pewter box and is based on a design created by Janet Edmunds.

Book cover and book mark

The instructions given below can be used to make a cover for any book. Simply adjust the measurements and quantities of materials given. The inner flap on the book cover made here is approximately 6cm (2¼in) but this measurement should be increased for a larger book. It is suggested that you read through all the instructions before embarking on this project so that you are familiar with the choices given in some of the steps.

Book cover

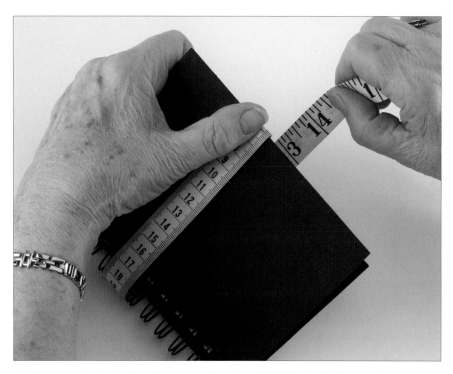

1. Measure the book, allowing an extra 2 x 6cm (2¼in) for inside flaps and an extra 6mm (¼in) at the top and the bottom. For the A6 book used in this project, this makes a total size of 40 x 17cm (15¾ x 6¾in).

Materials

For the book cover:

Ringbound A6 sketchbook

Black felt, 40 x 17cm (15¾ x 6¾in)

Two pieces of bump, each 16 x 12cm (6¼ x 4¾in)

Two pieces of pewter, at least 14 x 10cm (5½ x 4in)

One piece of torn silver metallic silk gauze, 6 x 17cm (2¼ x 6¾in), and another piece 7 x 7cm (2¾ x 2¾in)

Multicoloured decorative metallic thread

Silver and black variegated metallic machine embroidery thread

Silver metallic machine embroidery thread

(The fancy cord, see step 11, is made from three lengths of decorative embroidery thread.)

Black sewing thread

All-purpose glue

Tape measure

Embossing tool

Biro

Old scissors for cutting metal, or craft knife and cutting mat

Ruler

Mouse mat or cutting mat

Fabric scissors

Small pair of embroidery scissors

For the book mark:

Pewter, 4.5 x 18cm (1¾ x 7in)

Bump, minimum 6 x 20cm (2¼ x 7¾in)

Vilene (craft interfacing), painted with silver ink, 4.5 x 18cm (1¾ x 7in)

Silver metallic silk gauze, 4.5 x 4.5cm (1¾in)

48cm (19in) fancy cord, as above

Temporary adhesive spray

Tools and threads as for the book cover

2. Use these measurements to make a rectangular paper template, pin it to the black felt and cut out the rectangle.

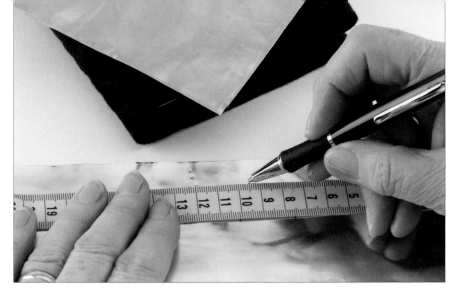

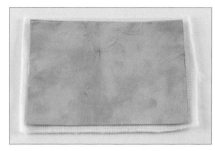

3. Wrap the felt around the book and measure the size required for the pewter panels on the front and back of the cover. These should not lie too close to the edges of the cover. The panels used here measure 9.5 x 14cm (3¾ x 5½in). Cut two pieces of pewter to the correct size, having marked the outline of the rectangle with a biro. These panels can be cut with a pair of old scissors for cutting metal or with a craft knife on a craft mat.

4. Cut two pieces of bump (or other backing fabric), each slightly larger than the pewter to allow for some movement during stitching.

5. Emboss the flower design (or a design of your choice) on to one of the pieces of pewter, placing it in the middle horizontally and slightly higher than the centre vertically. Rest the pewter on a mouse mat or craft mat and draw the design freehand using an embossing tool. Alternatively, a design can be traced if preferred.

6. Lay the pewter with the design drawn on over a piece of bump backing slightly larger than the pewter and place the smaller piece of silver metallic gauze over the design. Free machine stitch around the design using a silver and black metallic thread.

7. Using a small pair of embroidery scissors, trim away the silver metallic gauze from around the outline of the design, being careful not to damage the stitching.

8. Change to a silver metallic thread and free machine stitch over the rest of the pewter. Trim off the excess bump backing.

9. Rest the second piece of pewter on the second piece of bump backing and make a random but neat pattern of indentations over the surface using an embossing tool. This technique is known as pouncing.

10. Stitch the pewter to the bump backing by straight stitching around the perimeter approximately 3mm (1/8in) from the edge of the pewter. Trim off the excess bump backing.

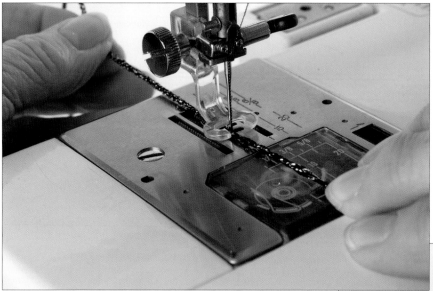

11. Make the decorative cord: for this book cover you will need 118cm (46½in) to go around the outside edge of the black felt rectangle, 103cm (40½in) for the two pewter panels and 122cm (48in) for the seven lengths that decorate the spine. This makes a total length of approximately 343cm (135in). To make the cord use three lengths of multicoloured decorative metallic thread stitched together using silver and black variegated metallic machine embroidery thread (see page 116 for instructions on making cords).

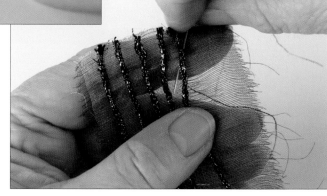

12. Measure a piece of silver metallic gauze that is the same width and length as the spine. This book cover requires a piece 6 x 17cm (2¼ x 6¾in). Do not cut out this rectangle with a pair of scissors but tear down each side of the metallic silk gauze to create a frayed edge. Cut seven lengths of cord, each one the same length as the spine, spacing them equidistantly across the width of the gauze and using a few holding stitches to keep them in place, lightly hand stitched using the black and silver thread.

80

13. Measure the exact middle of the book cover and place the gauze down the centre of the felt to form the spine. Machine stitch over each of the cords using a zig-zag stitch with the silver and black metallic thread.

14. Using wide spacing, hand stitch the cord into place around the perimeter of the black felt using black thread (this will be machine stitched over later). This light hand stitching will hold the cord in place and prevent any stretching when machine stitching along the edge later.

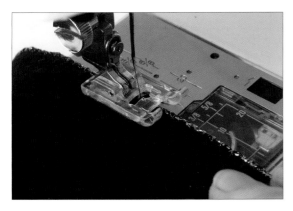

15. Using a zig-zag machine stitch and the black and silver machine embroidery thread, attach the cord to the felt. Stitch over the hand stitching, which will then be concealed.

16. Take each piece of decorated pewter for the panels and, very slightly, gently bend in the edge of the pewter to make a soft, rounded edge. Attach the two pewter panels to the front and back of the book cover using all-purpose glue. Oversew the cord around the edge of each panel using black thread, keeping very close to the edge of the pewter. Alternatively, the cord can be attached to the pewter panels using a zig-zag machine stitch and a silver metallic thread before attaching the panels to the felt. You may prefer not to attach a cord at all, which was my original intention, but I feel the addition of the decorative cord gives the book cover a more finished appearance.

17. Fold the inner flaps in on to the inside of the book cover and, using a zig-zag machine stitch and the silver and black variegated metallic machine embroidery thread, stitch along the whole length of the top and bottom edges of the black felt, not just along the edges of the flaps.

The finished book cover. The pewter panel could be made smaller but this size of panel gives stability to the felt. Painted Vilene could be an alternative to the black felt and this would make a more solid background material for the cover if smaller pieces of pewter were preferred.

Book mark

1. Resting on a mouse mat or craft mat, lay the pewter on the piece of bump backing and emboss the flower design on to the pewter using an embossing tool. (If you chose an alternative design for the book cover then use the same design for the book mark.)

2. Lay a piece of silver metallic gauze over the design and stitch it in place following the same method as used on the book cover (see step 6, page 79).

3. Cut away the excess gauze using a pair of sharp embroidery scissors.

4. Free machine stitch over the rest of the pewter using silver metallic machine embroidery thread.

5. Trim off the excess bump backing. Make a 48cm (19in) length of the same cord you used on the cover, and use a zig-zag stitch to attach the cord in place around the perimeter of the book mark.

6. Attach the silver-painted Vilene to the back of the pewter and backing using temporary adhesive spray, and machine stitch it in place using a zig-zag stitch with silver thread.

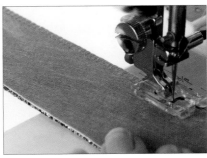

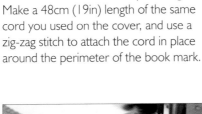

This book mark is large enough to be used with a larger sketchbook or any other size book you may wish to make.

Decorative stitching

Many very pleasing effects can be achieved by using decorative automatic machine stitches on metal. Care should be taken when choosing an automatic stitch to ensure there are not too many stitches close together as this could result in a pile of stitches on top of each other and a large hole in the metal. It is always wise to experiment on a small piece of metal before embarking on a project. Simple automatic machine stitches can be stitched on metal in lines, which can then be cut into strips and used to weave, as shown on page 100.

Decorative automatic stitches are extremely effective when making braids, edgings and tassels (see pages 112 to 119). The use of bright coloured rayon or metallic machine embroidery threads will make a dramatic statement, though the effect of using paler or variegated threads is more subtle, but no less effective. The use of automatic stitches when preparing a background for additional decoration, where the thread used blends into the fabric and fibres, can be seen in the photograph below.

A layer of velvet with painted Bondaweb (fusible adhesive mesh) applied has been covered with a sheet of copper foil, a layer of multicoloured Angelina and two layers of black chiffon. After a short application of heat from a heat gun it was then stitched diagonally with different automatic stitches and a number of different machine embroidery threads. The finished piece has a highly textured, coloured surface.

This is a detail of the Seedhead Vessel shown on page 89; the decorative automatic machine stitches can be seen clearly on the yellow silk and the copper wire mesh.

Seedhead vessel

This delicate, ornamental vessel resembles the seedhead of an exotic flower, hence its name. It is made of copper wire mesh and silk, decorated with a decorative automatic machine stitch. For the project piece I have used a commercial ribbon and cord; the second example, shown on page 89, uses torn strips of metallic silk gauze as a ribbon and a hand-made cord of several threads.

Templates

The templates provided below are reproduced two-thirds actual size and therefore need to be enlarged by fifty per cent.

Materials

Shot silk in shades of pink, orange and yellow, minimum 24 x 17cm (9½ x 6¾in)

Copper wire mesh, minimum 24 x 14cm (9½ x 5½in)

200cm (79in) of decorative silk ribbon

100cm (39½in) of cord to match or complement the silk

Pink enamelled 28g copper wire

Variegated polyneon machine embroidery thread

Copper metallic machine embroidery thread

Knitting needle, size 3mm

Scissors for cutting metal

Fabric scissors

Pins

Sewing needle

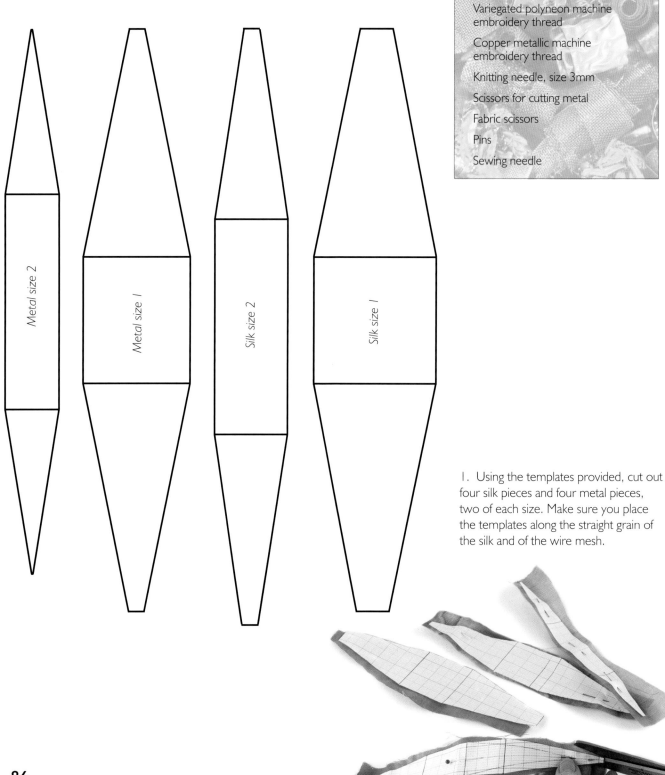

Metal size 2

Metal size 1

Silk size 2

Silk size 1

1. Using the templates provided, cut out four silk pieces and four metal pieces, two of each size. Make sure you place the templates along the straight grain of the silk and of the wire mesh.

2. Cut four lengths of decorative silk ribbon each 24cm (9½in) long and pin them along each side of the two larger silk pieces, placing them slightly in from the edge. Tack the ribbon in place.

3. Pin one of the larger wire mesh shapes to the front of each of the two larger silk shapes, partially covering the ribbon. Machine stitch the wire mesh in place around the edge using a decorative automatic machine stitch and a variegated polyneon embroidery thread (or a thread of your choice). Resist trimming off any stray threads if the edge of the fabric begins to fray as this will add to the character of the finished piece. Try to use only two pins at the most and position them where the holes will be hidden.

4. Remove the pins and the tacking stitches and lay one of the larger shapes at right angles across the other one with the right sides (metal sides) facing down, as shown in the photograph. Using one pin only, pin the two shapes together, avoiding passing the pin through the wire mesh of the outer layer.

5. Turn the shapes over so that the right sides are facing up and, using just a few stitches, hand sew them together at the four corners where they cross using copper metallic thread. Pass the needle through the same holes as the decorative stitching on the wire mesh surface.

6. Repeat steps 2 to 5 using the narrower shapes and 24cm (9½in) lengths of ribbon. Cut two lengths of decorative cord, each slightly longer than the shapes, and wrap each piece of cord with a length of thin enamelled wire, as illustrated.

7. On the fabric side of each narrower shape oversew by hand a length of cord down the centre using copper metallic thread. Ensure the needle does not pass through the wire mesh underneath.

8. Sew the two narrower shapes together using the same method as before (steps 4 and 5). Start to bend the petals upwards with the metal layers on the outside. Curl the tips of the petals outwards around a knitting needle.

9. Form the larger pieces into the shape of the vessel with the wire mesh layers on the outside. Curl the tips of the petals outwards around a knitting needle, as before.

10. Continue sculpting both the larger pieces and the narrower pieces until you are happy with their shapes. Place the narrower pieces inside the larger, offsetting them so that the inner petals lie in the gaps between the outer ones.

11. Turn the vessel over and attach the two pieces together using small stitches placed at each corner of the square base. Use copper thread and pass the needle through the same holes as the existing stitching. Adjust the shapes of the petals if required.

The finished vessel, made using commercial variegated knitting ribbon and cord. There is a hint of pink in the overall colour of this piece, resulting from the light reflecting off the pink area of the variegated ribbon and the heat-treated copper wire mesh having a slightly pink tinge.

This is a finished vessel, which has been made using a torn strip of pale blue silk metallic gauze and a more orange group of threads to make a cord. The copper wire mesh heat treatment has created a more blue and grey colour, which affects the overall colour of the vessel.

Embroidered cuff

This embroidered cuff demonstrates the use of silk rods with strips of decorative machine stitching on heat-treated copper wire mesh. Choose a colour from the many pre-dyed silk rods available and paint or dye a piece of Vilene (craft interfacing) to match. The lining fabric can be a metallic silk or any smooth fabric to complement the colour of the silk rods. The lining used for this project is bronze metallic silk.

The measurements given in the materials list are for an average size wrist; these should be adapted to fit the circumference of your own wrist. The depth of the cuff is 5cm (2in) but if you have a particularly small, delicate wrist you may wish to reduce this.

Materials

Bronze metallic silk fabric for lining, 7 x 22.5cm (2¾ x 9in)

Two pieces of Vilene (craft interfacing), 5 x 20cm (2 x 7¾in)

Two or three ready-dyed silk rods

Heat-treated copper wire mesh, minimum 5 x 12cm (2 x 4¾in)

Temporary adhesive spray

Variegated metallic machine embroidery thread

Copper metallic machine embroidery thread

Velcro (hook and loop fastener), 1.5 x 3cm (¾ x 1¼in)

Watercolour paint to match silk rods and a paintbrush

Graph paper (for template)

Pins

Scissors for cutting metal

Fabric scissors

Small pair of sharp embroidery scissors

Sewing needle

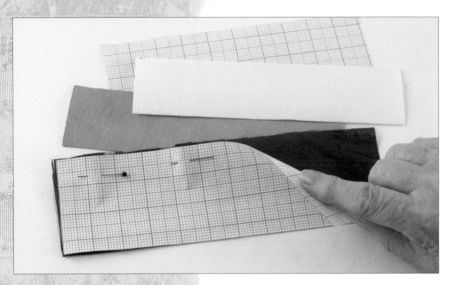

1. Measure the circumference of your wrist and add on 5cm (2in). Cut out a piece of bronze lining fabric that is this length and 7cm (2¾in) deep. You may prefer to use a template, as shown in the photograph above, which you can make easily from graph paper. Also cut out two pieces of Vilene that are 2.5cm (1in) shorter than the lining and approximately 5cm (2in) deep. Paint one of the pieces of Vilene using watercolour paints to match the colour of the silk rods.

2. Soak the silk rods in water for a few minutes until they are pliable and carefully peel off several fine layers.

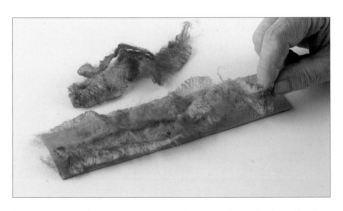

3. Lay some of the silk rod pieces in rows along the length of the coloured Vilene.

4. Pin and tack these pieces in position.

5. Cut eight strips of heat-treated copper wire mesh, each approximately 5cm (2in) long and 1.5cm (¾in) wide. Place a line of decorative automatic machine stitching down the centre of each piece using a variegated metallic thread. Change to copper metallic thread and attach each wire mesh strip to a piece of silk rod by straight machine stitching around the edge of the wire mesh.

6. Using the variegated thread, attach the silk rod strips you tacked to the Vilene earlier by straight stitching around the edge and in three rows lengthways.

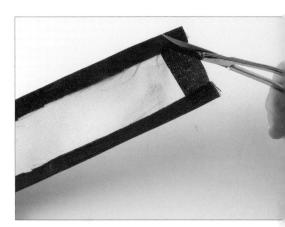

7. Apply temporary adhesive spray to the perimeter of the unpainted Vilene and lay it adhesive side up on the bronze silk. Fold the long edges of the bronze silk over the Vilene on to the spray adhesive and snip off the corners using a pair of sharp embroidery scissors. Fold the silk over the ends of the Vilene, adding more spray adhesive where fabric touches fabric.

8. Place the bronze silk-covered Vilene face down on the back of the red cuff and straight stitch it in place around the edge using copper metallic thread.

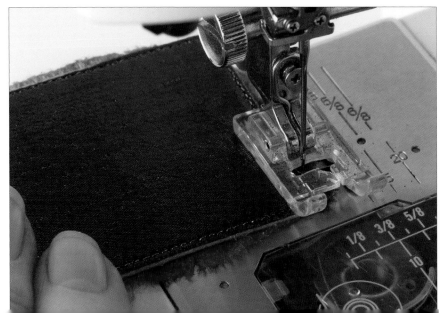

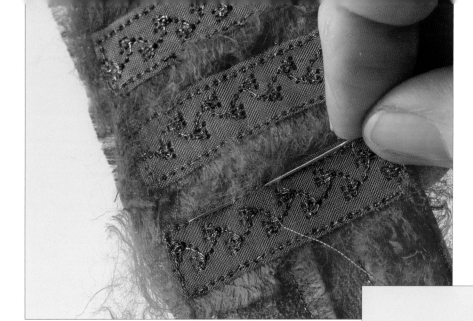

9. Attach each of the embroidered wire mesh and silk rod strips to the front of the cuff by hand, placing them in a row along its length with the fluffy edges pushed tightly together. Use copper thread and work the holding stitches into the machine stitching holes. Do not go right through the cuff to the lining but keep your stitches within the layers of silk rods.

10. Sew the short strips of Velcro (hook and loop fastener) to the back of one end of the cuff and the front of the other end to fasten the cuff around your wrist.

The finished cuff.

This cuff is made using the same method but is shorter in length as it has a bead and loop fastening instead of an overlap. The lining is a silver metallic silk fabric and the covering for the front is of black velvet with small squares of pewter prepared in the same way as for the pendant and the boxes on previous pages.

Woven strips

Weaving strips of metal can produce different results depending on the method used, as the three examples shown here demonstrate. The quirky metal doll has a body of evenly woven adhesive copper strips. All the strips are the same size and the weaving is regular, smooth and even. Instructions for making this doll, including details of how to weave the metal strips, are given on pages 104 to 109.

These woven metal strips show an assortment of surface finishes and were placed on a background of the reverse side of a piece of furnishing fabric. The horizontal strips, from top to bottom, are: the matt side of copper foil, which was heat-treated, painted with a red dye and then free machine stitched; fine copper foil with blue-painted Fibretex placed on top and a flower design free machine stitched on before the application of heat from a heat gun (most of the Fibretex has disappeared); heat-treated copper wire mesh, which was sprayed with gold webbing spray; and fine copper foil with blue-painted Fibretex, but this time a more dense design of free machining has prevented most of the Fibretex from being removed when it was heat-treated.

The vertical strips, from left to right, are: the matt side of copper foil that was heat-treated until a strong colour was achieved, then had foiling glue piped on and, when dry, was decorated with foil and rubbed with blue polish using a finger; a piece of heavy copper shim, embossed, with different coloured polishes rubbed on; the same metal and technique as the first vertical strip with a slightly different design.

This woven panel was started in a different way from the example above. A rectangle of copper shim was heat-treated and decorated with painted Bondaweb (fusible adhesive mesh), which was ironed on. Vertical strips 1cm (½in) wide were cut, starting at the bottom of the rectangle and stopping 1.5cm (¾in) below the top. Using 1, 1.5 and 2cm (½, ¾ and 1in) strips of various metals with different finishes, alternate vertical strips were raised up and the first horizontal strip woven into position at the top of the panel. These vertical strips were then laid back in place, the other alternate strips were raised, and the next horizontal strip was woven through. This process was repeated down the length of the rectangle of copper.

Woven Bowl

19 x 16 x 5cm (7½ x 6¼ x 2in)

Heat-treated strips of copper wire mesh, matt copper foil and copper shim were woven together, then placed on a backing of black Kunin felt. Black chiffon was placed over the metal and a meandering free machine stitch using a variegated black and gold metallic machine embroidery thread held the layers together. A craft gun was directed over the chiffon to partially disintegrate it. The bowl was then turned over and heat was concentrated on to the felt on the reverse side of the bowl. This succeeded in dissolving part of the felt to create a lacy effect. While still warm, the corners of the rectangle were pinched together and the sides raised to create a decorative bowl. Once cold, the bowl held its shape.

Woven panel

This decorative woven panel represents another method of weaving. It measures 15 x 21cm (6 x 8¼in) and can be mounted and framed in any style you choose, for example in a wooden box frame or attached to an artist's stretched canvas which has been painted with copper metallic paint. As with all the projects in this book, the colours, materials and methods you use can be varied – do not be afraid to experiment.

Template

The template provided below is reproduced two-thirds actual size and therefore needs to be enlarged by fifty per cent. The dashed lines represent the stitching lines.

Materials

Black felt, approximately
25 x 17cm (9¾ x 6¾in)

Sheet of fine copper foil,
22 x 15cm (8¾ x 6in)

Sheet of made Angelina,
22 x 15cm (8¾ x 6in)

Two pieces of black chiffon,
approximately 25 x 17cm
(9¾ x 6¾in)

Pewter, minimum 23 x 12cm
(9 x 4¾in), painted using dark pink
and purple spirit dyes

Heat-treated copper wire mesh,
21 x 10cm (8¼ x 4in)

Heat-treated brass wire mesh,
21 x 10cm (8¼ x 4in)

(The quantities given above
provide a little extra metal in case
of mistakes.)

Pink enamelled 28g copper wire

Variegated machine
embroidery thread

Copper metallic machine
embroidery thread

Heat gun

Pins

Scissors for cutting metal

Fabric scissors

Sewing needle

Ruler or tape measure

1. Create the background by layering black felt, fine copper foil, a sheet of Angelina and finally a double layer of black chiffon.

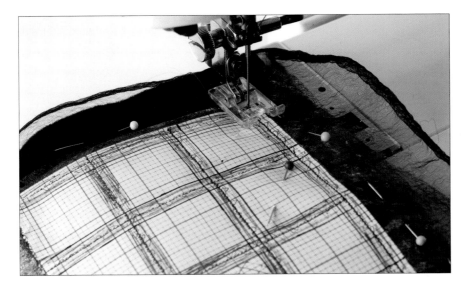

2. Pin the materials together around the four edges and pin the template in place in the centre. Position about six pins diagonally on the squares to avoid the stitching lines. Machine stitch along the dashed lines using a straight stitch and a variegated machine embroidery thread. These lines of stitching will be used to indicate where to position the strips of metal once the template has been removed.

3. Remove the paper template by carefully tearing it away from the stitched lines.

4. Remove the pins and heat the chiffon with a heat gun, initially held 10–12cm (4–4¾in) above the fabric and lowering it to 7–8cm (2¾–3¼in) if necessary, until it starts to disintegrate.

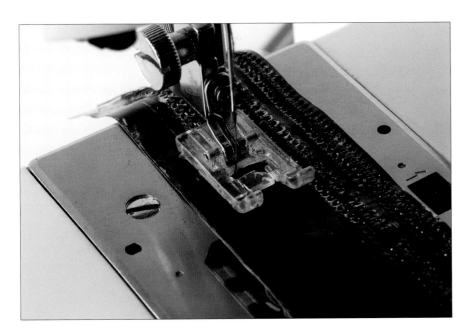

6. Cut out the strips between the lines of stitching. You will need seven 15cm (6in) long strips and five 22cm (8¾in) long strips.

5. Using the decorative automatic machine stitch of your choice, start stitching lines down the length of the purple-painted pewter. Leave sufficient space between the rows of stitching for the pewter to be cut into strips 0.8cm (½in) wide.

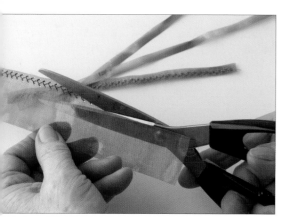  

7. Stitch along the length of heat-treated copper wire mesh several times using a decorative automatic machine stitch, and cut it into strips as in step 6. Cut the heat-treated brass wire mesh into strips of the same width but without stitching.

8. Attach the purple pewter strips to the background fabric using the stitched lines for guidance. (The stitched lines should be exactly underneath the middle of the pewter strips.) Begin by laying a 15cm (6in) strip along the top and a 22cm (8¾in) strip down the left-hand side. Secure them at the corner by hand using the existing machine-made holes.

9. Position a second vertical strip along the stitching line, this time laying it underneath the horizontal strip. Continue in this manner across the width of the panel, placing the verticals along the stitching lines and alternately over and under the top horizontal. Trim off the ends of the strips where necessary.

10. When the vertical strips are in place, trim off the excess backing fabrics and start to attach the remaining horizontal strips. Weave in and out of the vertical strips and secure them at each junction using hand stitching worked through the existing machine-made holes. Secure the last corner to complete the weaving of the pewter strips.

11. Lay the stitched copper wire mesh strips diagonally across the panel and secure them by hand where they cross the purple strips using a copper metallic thread. Trim the ends of the strips parallel with the edge of the panel.

12. Lay the brass wire mesh strips diagonally in the other direction, weaving them in and out of the copper strips and trimming the ends as before. Secure them at each end using a very fine, pink enamelled wire. Thread a sewing needle with the wire and take it through the fabric from the front to the back, then back through to the front, leaving two 2.5cm (1in) tails. Twist these two ends together tightly, separate them, and curl them round a bodkin to make a decorative coil.

13. Make two small beads using remnants of the stitched copper wire mesh strips and attach them to two opposite corners of the panel.

The completed panel.

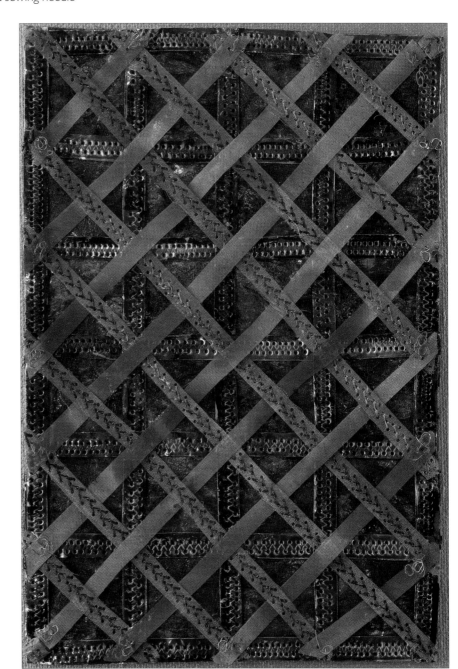

Greetings cards

Decorated metal can be used to make an endless variety of unusual greetings cards. An interesting design can be made using woven strips and hand-made beads (see page 114). Blank greetings cards can be bought from most art and craft shops and vary in size, colour and design. Some have an aperture in the middle of a two-fold card, an example of which can be seen on page 103 at the top of the group of finished cards.

The instructions given below are for a woven design of strips of copper wire mesh.

1. Cut seven 1.5cm (¾in) wide strips of heat-treated copper wire mesh, three 8.5cm (3½in) long and four 6.5cm (2½in) long. Using a decorative automatic machine stitch, sew a line down the centre of each strip using a variegated metallic thread.

2. Starting at the top, attach three long vertical strips to a short horizontal strip, placing the two outer strips underneath the horizontal and the middle one on top. Secure the strips using small holding stitches worked over the existing machine stitching using copper thread. Work the copper thread across the front from one junction to the next rather than cutting it off each time, thereby creating a decorative surface grid. Weave the remaining three short strips through the verticals, pinning them all in place before securing them in the same way as the first strips.

3. Curl small pieces of heat-treated copper shim round a knitting needle to make beads and attach them to the woven design using copper wire. Thread a needle with the copper wire and insert the needle from the back to the front of the design, pass it through the bead and take it down to the back.

4. Twist the ends of the wire together at the back to secure the bead, leaving long tail threads to create additional decoration. These ends can be slightly curled and will show below the woven panel, or above and to the side if you wish.

5. Stitch the woven wire mesh to the front of the card, placing a single holding stitch in each corner using the needle still threaded with the copper wire. Work the stitches so that the two tail threads are on the front. Twist the tail threads together to secure them, then open out the ends, cut them to about 2.5cm (1in) and curl them into a decorative finish.

The finished card, together with cards of other designs using techniques shown elsewhere in the book.

Top: using a two-fold card with an aperture, a piece of crumpled copper has been treated with painted Tyvek and machine stitched around some of the crease lines. The Tyvek was then heat-treated to almost destruction point. A few beads were hand sewn to add interest.

Middle: heat-treated copper wire mesh was stitched on to a light-weight backing using a scroll design. Beads were added and the piece was then attached to black felt using a decorative scalloped automatic machine stitch around the edge to merge the copper into the felt. The felt was then cut out around the stitch line and a wire mesh bead was attached at the bottom of the design. The black felt was fixed to a piece of purple hand-made paper which was then fixed to the card by permanent spray adhesive.

Bottom: this card was made of creased, heat-treated matt copper foil with Pebeo puff paint piped around the lines created by the heat treatment. Permanent spray adhesive was used to fix the metal to a piece of black felt before free machine stitching beside the paint lines. Silver polish was rubbed over the creases in the metal and the puff paint, and finally the black felt was attached to the card with spray adhesive.

Quirky metal doll

This eye-catching doll has a body made of woven adhesive copper foil strips. Making the woven body can be a time-consuming, though worthwhile, exercise, so as an alternative to the copper strips a rectangle of heat-treated copper wire mesh decorated with machine stitching could be used instead. You would need a piece measuring 17 x 11.5cm (6¾ x 4½in). This would alter the character of the doll but would allow a more quirky head, or quirky arms and legs, to be considered.

This doll has 'attitude', partly because she has no neck, which affects the position of her head. If required, a neck could be added to give the doll a more upright appearance, but this would remove some of her quirkiness.

Templates

The templates provided below are reproduced half actual size and therefore need to be doubled.

Materials

Furnishing fabric (use a fabric which frays easily), four pieces 6 x 9cm (2¼ x 3½in) for legs and one piece at least 17 x 11.5cm (6¾ x 4½in) for the body

Small quantity of SMA polyester filling

Heat-treated fine woven copper cloth, one piece 7 x 5.5cm (2¾ x 2¼in) for face and two pieces 2 x 3cm (¾ x 1¼in) for shoulders

Heat-treated copper wire mesh, one piece 30 x 7cm (11¾ x 2¾in) for hair and two pieces 10 x 2cm (4 x ¾in) for legs

Roll of tubular copper knitted wire, 1.5cm (¾in) wide

Calico, minimum 18 x 13cm (7 x 5in)

Bronze silk metallic gauze (for head), two pieces 7 x 5.5cm (2¾ x 2¼in)

Self-adhesive copper foil tape, 0.6cm (¼in) wide

Variegated metallic machine embroidery thread

Copper metallic machine embroidery thread

Knitting needle, size 3mm

Beads – two tiny beads for the eyes, two coiled decorative beads and about 20 small, coloured metallic beads for decoration

Double-sided adhesive tape

Small quantity of 28g copper wire

Scissors for cutting metal

Fabric scissors

Ruler or tape measure

Sewing needle

Pins

Body (calico), 18 x 13cm (7 x 5in)

Body (furnishing fabric), 17 x 11.5cm (6¾ x 4½in)

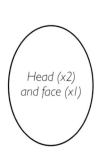

Head (x2) and face (x1)

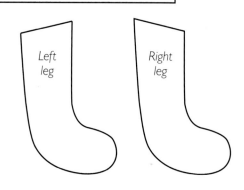

Left leg

Right leg

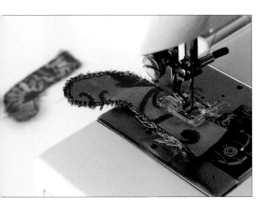

1. Using double-thickness furnishing fabric, cut out the two legs. Straight stitch the two layers of fabric together round the edge using a variegated metallic thread. Strengthen the outer edge by using a zig-zag stitch, which will reinforce the straight stitching. Do not worry if the furnishing fabric starts to fray – it will only fray up to the double row of stitching and it will add to the character of the finished doll.

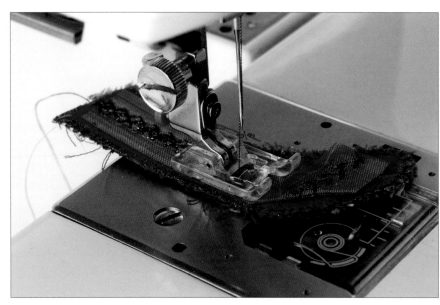

2. Take two lengths of heat-treated copper wire mesh, each approximately 10 x 2cm (4 x ¾in). Sew a line of decorative automatic machine stitching down the centre of each strip using the variegated thread. Attach a wire mesh strip to each of the doll's legs using a smaller version of the same decorative automatic machine stitch (going over the existing larger stitches), folding one end of the wire mesh over to match the shape of the foot.

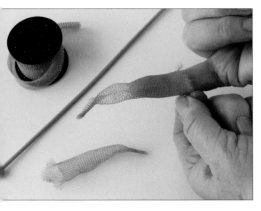

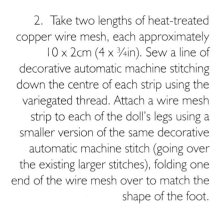

4. Using copper wire, attach a small, coloured metallic bead to the tightly closed end of each arm. Leave long tail threads, which you will use later to attach the arms to the doll's body.

3. For the arms, cut two lengths of tubular copper knitted wire mesh, each 10cm (4in) long. Open up the tubes with a knitting needle and then, using your finger, enlarge the opening to the size you want. Press the sides of one end closely together.

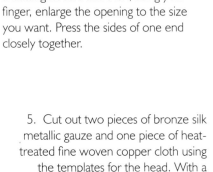

5. Cut out two pieces of bronze silk metallic gauze and one piece of heat-treated fine woven copper cloth using the templates for the head. With a narrow seam, sew the two gauze pieces together by hand, using copper thread and leaving the neck end open. Stuff the head with SMA polyester filling.

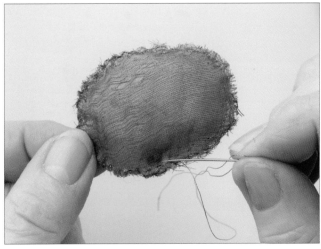

7. Using the variegated metallic thread, stitch on the features of the face by hand. The mouth is made with two long stitches starting in the middle of the mouth. You can define the mood of the doll by the shape of the mouth. The eyebrows and nose are constructed in the same way. Two small beads are used for the eyes. Sew each of the stitches twice with double thread for additional strength.

6. Sew up the neck and attach the heat-treated fine woven copper to one side of the head to form the face.

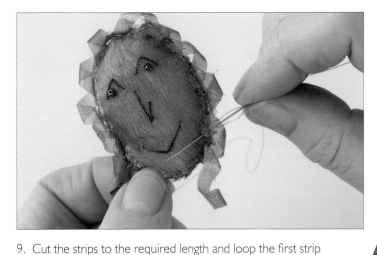

8. For the hair, cut thin strips of heat-treated copper wire mesh approximately 30 x 0.5cm (11¾ x ¼in) and twist them around a knitting needle.

9. Cut the strips to the required length and loop the first strip around the head so that it covers the seam and frames the face.

10. Cut out a piece of calico for the doll's body using the template provided. Fold the calico in half with right sides together and sew up the side and base. Trim off the stitched corners diagonally, turn it the right side out and fill the body with the SMA polyester filling. Push it down firmly with the end of a knitting needle. Fold in the cut edge of the calico by approximately 1cm (½in).

11. Insert the tops of the legs in the open end of the body, pin them in place and sew across the seam by hand using the copper thread. Manipulate the legs in place to achieve a walking position.

12. Attach the head to the top of the body using hand stitching at the base of the head. Ensure that the head is able to be moved slightly into position when the outer metal body is put in place, adding a few more stitches then to stabilise it if necessary. Slight movement of the head is part of the doll's attraction. Position the head so that the chin slightly overlaps the front of the body. Tilt it a little to one side to give the doll more character.

13. Cut out the rectangle of furnishing fabric using the template provided, lay it so that the longest sides run widthways and cut an 18cm (7in) long strip of self-adhesive copper foil tape. Peel a little of the backing away from the copper and attach the strip to the top left-hand corner of the fabric so that it runs from left to right. Cut two further strips of copper tape approximately 12cm (4¾in) long and attach these to the left-hand end of the first strip and at right angles to it, as shown in the photograph above. Place the first vertical strip on top of the horizontal and the second strip underneath it to create the start of the woven pattern. Make sure you only peel away enough of the backing to secure the strips to each other; only the horizontal strip has alternate strips adhering to the furnishing fabric at this stage.

14. Continue working the woven design across and downwards, alternately adding horizontal and vertical strips. Try to keep the copper strips parallel, with no gaps in between. Once anchored securely at the sides of the fabric, there is no need to stick the strips down along their entire length. Simply weave each one through the existing strips, securing them to the furnishing fabric at random intervals in the centre by removing a piece of the backing. Secure them completely when you are within two or three centimetres of the edge.

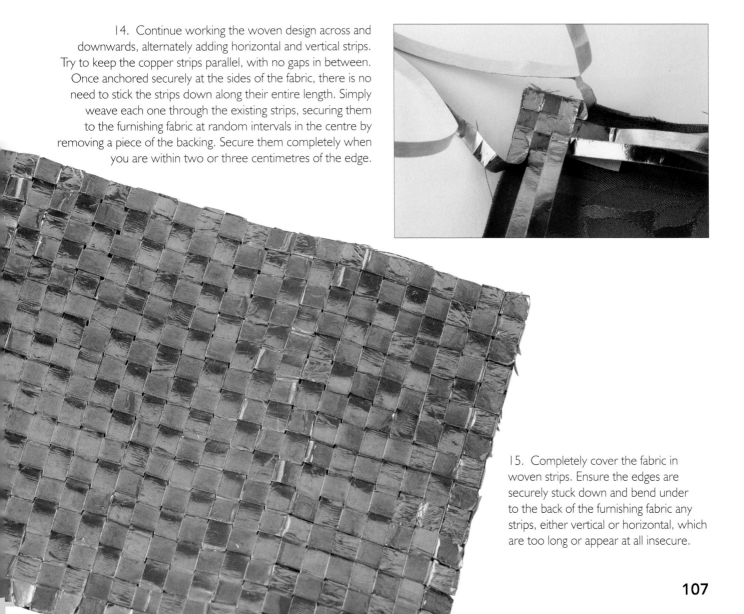

15. Completely cover the fabric in woven strips. Ensure the edges are securely stuck down and bend under to the back of the furnishing fabric any strips, either vertical or horizontal, which are too long or appear at all insecure.

16. Wrap the sheet of woven copper strips around the calico body to find the correct position for the two decorative beads. Bring the copper thread up to the front of the copper sheet, thread on a coiled bead then a smaller bead, take the thread back through the coiled bead and secure it on the back of the furnishing fabric.

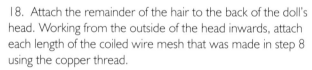

17. Attach a length of double-sided adhesive tape down the inside edge of one of the ends of the woven copper sheet and wrap the woven sheet around the calico body so that the seam is at the back. Remove the tape backing and secure the metal sheet firmly, holding it in place for a few minutes until you are satisfied that it has stuck permanently.

18. Attach the remainder of the hair to the back of the doll's head. Working from the outside of the head inwards, attach each length of the coiled wire mesh that was made in step 8 using the copper thread.

19. Sew on the arms using the same thread used for attaching the beads, passing it through both the woven copper sheet and the calico to strengthen the join.

20. Seal the seam on the back of the doll's body using a strip of self-adhesive copper foil tape.

21. Cut two small strips of heat-treated fine woven copper and fold them over the shoulders. Oversew them in place using variegated metallic machine embroidery thread, working first in one direction and then in the other to strengthen the stitching. This will also create a decorative stitch. Finally, secure the head at an angle using a few hidden stitches.

22. Sew up the seam along the base of the body, at the same time stitching on small metallic coloured beads at regular intervals. Use the variegated thread.

Demon of Despair

This doll, known as the Demon of Despair, is one of a pair. It represents the black mood of a child and is in contrast to the Happy Sprite when the child is happy and carefree (not shown). The face is covered by a mask, which hides the child's true feelings, and the untouchable, prickly hair is made of fine, twisted, wrapped (stitched) wire. Even the wings are made of knitted crinkled wire and are a warning that she is not to be touched! A breastplate of machine-stitched charcoal metallic thread conceals the true emotions of the heart. Metal armature supports the body, with wadding wrapped around followed by strips of a plain jersey cotton. Finally, strips of a decorative fabric are wound around and stitched in place at intervals.

Facing page (anticlockwise, beginning top left): the facemask is made of Fimo soft polymer modelling clay, with a furrowed brow and other facial features created using sequins and beads embedded in the Fimo; the breastplate shows layers of free machine stitching on water-soluble film; the feet are encased in shoes made of Fimo and held in place by fine brass wire; the hair is made of wrapped (stitched) brass wire, wound around a knitting needle to achieve the spiky ringlets.

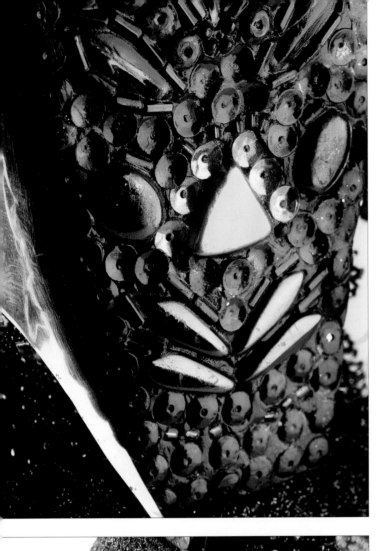

Embellishments

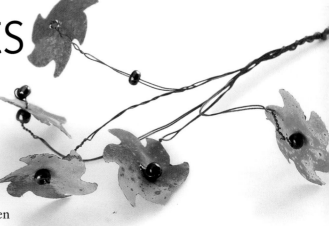

Braids, edgings, beads and tassels made of metal can be used in the same way as embellishments made of fabric. Craft punches can be used to cut out shapes with ease from metal foil. The shapes can be used to decorate work, applied under chiffon or gauze or used as flowers with wire and beads. Tassels can provide added interest when made of metal and used in conjunction with tassels of thread or fabric (see vessel on page 116).

Most embellishments can be made of small off-cuts of metal. Never throw away small strips or odd shapes. It is amazing how often they can be recycled into something useful.

Edgings and braids

Edgings and braids can be made in many different widths and styles to add interest to a piece of work. The photographs below show three methods of making them but as the photograph on the facing page shows, there are endless variations.

The photograph opposite illustrates the variety of edgings and braids that can be made.

Place a strip of heat-treated wire mesh over a strip of metallic striped gauze and stitch down the centre using a decorative automatic machine embroidery stitch worked in silver metallic thread.

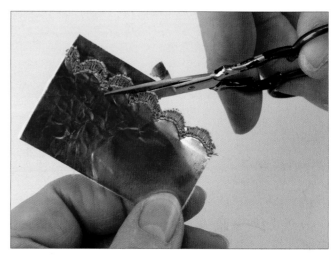

A decorative automatic machine embroidery stitch worked in a blue rayon machine embroidery thread along a piece of heat-treated copper shim can be used to make an effective edging. The unwanted metal is cut away from the stitching using a small, sharp pair of embroidery scissors, being careful not to cut any of the threads. The width of the edging can be varied depending on its intended use. For joining to other metals or fabrics there needs to be enough room to stitch the two items together. For a finer edging, a narrower strip can be used and attached by hand, stitching over the existing machine stitching.

Using a craft punch, cut out decorative shapes from a strip of heat-treated matt copper foil. As well as creating a colourful braid, the cut-out pieces can be used to make a tassel by threading them on to coloured wire or cord. With a small bead positioned in the centre of these cut-out pieces they can resemble flowers (shown top right).

112

Beads

Never throw away any pieces of metal, as even the smallest strips can be used to make a bead by rolling it around a knitting needle or a bodkin. For a larger bead use a larger knitting needle. A piece of metal in the shape of a long triangle, when rolled from the wide end towards the point, creates a bead that is round in the centre and tapers at each end. Beads can be used for decoration on a panel or to make jewellery, where care should be taken to avoid sharp edges next to the skin. The examples at the bottom of the page show beads made of copper shim, stamped wire mesh, wire and cord twisted around a knitting needle, beaded wire, wound wire, and copper wire mesh made with a long rectangular strip.

Winding wire

Using a wire winder achieves a tight spiral of wire, which can be cut up into short lengths to make beads or left longer for other embellishments. The wound wire can be either machine stitched with a zig-zag stitch or left unstitched, and made in two different sizes according to which winder is used. The spiral can be left tightly and evenly wound or, for a more decorative effect, it can be partially extended or twisted.

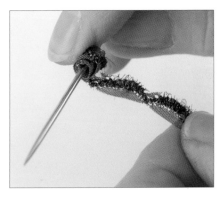

An example of an off-cut of a very narrow strip of edging being wound around a bodkin to create a bead.

A plain bead of a rolled, narrow strip of copper is decorated with a piece of machine-wrapped (stitched) wire wound around the outside five or six times.

Working directly from the reel of wire, secure the end of the wire to the wire winder and simply turn the handle. Ensure the twists are even, with no gaps in between.

The two wound wires shown here have been wound using the two different-sized winders – the black wire was made using the larger winder and has been stretched and manipulated. The silver wire, made with the thinner winder, has been left untouched.

Tassels

Metal tassels can be hung from the corners of a vessel in the same way as a fabric or thread tassel. In fact there is no reason why a metal tassel cannot be used in any situation where a tassel of any type will enhance your work. The samples to the right show a small selection of metal tassels. Ribbled metal is particularly effective, as are twisted wound wires and copper wire mesh triangles stitched over a hand-made cord. Stitched copper foil enclosed in plastic by using a laminator is another interesting technique.

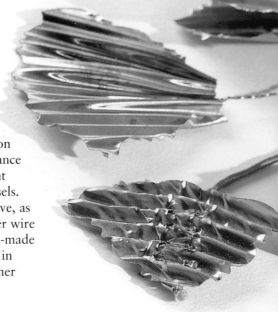

Left: a paper-wrapped wire frame supports decorated net panels with various tassels (metal, plastic, fabric and thread) hanging from each corner.

Cords

Cords are easy to make, consisting simply of several lengths of thread stitched together using a zig-zag machine stitch. They can be used to decorate a flat piece of work, such as that shown on page 118; to give a finished appearance to the edge of a three-dimensional item, for example a vessel, a box or a piece of jewellery, as shown in many of the preceding projects in this book; or used to attach tassels, as shown here.

Making a cord

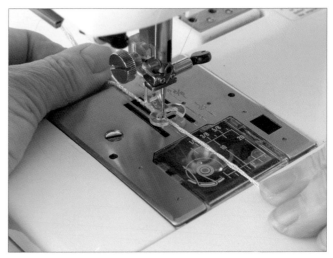

1. Twist three lengths of thread together and place them under the needle of your sewing machine. If a thicker cord is required use either thicker threads or more than three threads. The feed dog should be down, the darning foot or open toe foot in place and the presser foot down. Holding the machine threads out to the left and the cord taut, start to stitch using a zig-zag stitch for approximately 2.5cm (1in) along the length of the cord.

2. You should now be able to release the sewing thread and continue stitching to the end of the cord. Retain tension of the cord and twist the threads together as you work. By moving the cord along under the needle you can control whether the threads are fully or partially covered by the machine embroidery threads.

Stitching on wire

1. Drop the feed dog, put a darning foot or open toe foot on to the sewing machine and thread it with your chosen thread. Place a length of fine wire under the needle and put the presser foot down. Holding the machine threads out to the left and the wire taut from either end, start to zig-zag along the length using a slightly narrow width setting for the stitch.

2. Stitch smoothly along the length of the wire. The faster the movement of the wire under the needle the more spaced out will be the stitching. For complete coverage, move the wire along slowly under the needle.

Twisted Strips

This panel demonstrates the use of cords and stitched and plain wires. A background of purple Kunin felt displays two panels of gold metallic gauze, which have been applied with a decorative automatic machine embroidery stitch. A short burst of heat from a heat gun has distorted the gauze where there is no stitching. Strips of purple Kunin felt were twisted and wrapped with enamelled wire, and also with beaded and wrapped (stitched) wire, and applied by hand to the background. A selection of different coloured wrapped cords were threaded over and under the strips of felt.

Decorative finishes

Surface decoration on fabric can be used in the same way on metal. All the following materials and techniques are described on the preceding pages, and here they have been used together to create a decorative panel which is, at the same time, a record of the various effects that can be achieved. All the examples are applied to pewter and have a bump backing. The samples have been applied to a stretched canvas which has been covered with strong stainless steel woven cloth.

Key

 Lime green metallic paint was applied to one side of Tyvek and pink metallic paint to the other side. Three lines of diagonal stitching secured the Tyvek to the pewter, painted with lime green metallic paint. After heating the Tyvek to shrink it, a further two diagonal lines of stitching were applied to the pewter and a little pink metallic paint was rubbed on around the edges of the Tyvek.

 Water-soluble paper was moulded over an Indian printing block. When almost dry the mould was removed from the block and applied to the pewter, smoothing the dampened edges on to the metal. When dry it was painted using pink metallic paint, with lime green metallic paint in the recesses. Pink metallic paint was applied to the pewter and a layer of black chiffon stitched on with silver metallic thread using a meandering free machine stitch. A heat gun was used to remove the chiffon from the centre and around the edges.

 A leaf design was stitched on to water-soluble paper. This was then dampened, pressed on to the pewter, and the stitched leaf design exposed by removing some of the damp pulp. When the paper was completely dry, colour was applied to the leaf design and the area around it. Silver polish was rubbed on using a finger to complete the design.

 Two leaves were stitched on to painted Fibretex, which had first been placed on to the pewter. Heat was applied with a heat gun to disintegrate the Fibretex between the stitching, and a red shimmer pen was applied in the open spaces.

 Pink metallic gauze was stitched on to the pewter with meandering free machine stitching. A pewter flower was made, painted with a red shimmer pen and applied by hand with a bead in the centre.

 Purple spirit dyes were applied to the pewter. A decorative grid was stitched by machine on to water-soluble film, dissolved and the grid applied by hand.

 Painted Lutradur 70 was stamped with an Indian printing block, which was stitched around on to pewter painted with purple dye. The Lutradur was heated to remove the outer area around the stitching.

 Lime green metallic paint was applied to the pewter. Kunin felt was stitched on in a series of triangles, then heated to disintegrate it around the stitching. Red shimmer pen was applied lightly over the Kunin felt and the lime green paint.

 Painted Bondaweb was applied to the pewter. Painted Tyvek was stitched in a spiral design on to the pewter then heated to expose more of the stitching and the outer edges of the Bondaweb.

 Red shimmer pen was painted on to the pewter. Painted garden fleece was stitched on and then heated to reveal the painted background.

 Silver Sizoflor was stitched on to purple-painted pewter and heated to reveal the background.

 Deep pink chiffon was stitched on to the pewter background, lightly heated and red shimmer pen delicately applied.

Framed display of four decorative finishes

Four examples of decorative finishes are displayed here in a painted photograph frame. Each example shows a variation on the use of different surface finishes – the range of thicknesses and the resulting textures – on a background of heat-treated copper.

Garden fleece was painted with metallic paints and stitched to heat-treated copper foil using a flower design. After heating with a heat gun to partially disintegrate the garden fleece, further metallic paint was applied to highlight some areas. Beads were hand sewn on to the centre of the flowers.

Light-weight Lutradur 30 was coloured with red and brown dyes, free machined in spirals with a fine copper metallic machine embroidery thread and then heat was applied to partially disintegrate the surface. Gold polish was rubbed lightly with a finger over the raised areas, and the piece was then placed on a lightly heat-treated piece of copper foil, which gleams through the open areas with a rich, copper glow.

A heavier-weight Lutradur 70 was coloured with strong purple, brown and red dyes and, when dry, was stitched in a grid with copper metallic machine embroidery thread. Heat-treated matt copper foil squares were included in the grid stitching. When treated with a heat gun the Lutradur shrank, pulling the copper squares into creases. These were further scrunched by hand and the surface of the creases rubbed with copper polish. The background of copper shim was heat-treated to a strong reddish glow to appear through the gaps in the Lutradur.

The background of heat-treated copper shim is much darker on this sample than in the other three examples. The Lutradur 70 was painted and then free machine stitched with a few meandering lines before being lightly heated with a heat gun. This example has a chunkier texture, which was then rubbed with lime green and smokey blue metallic paint on the raised surface.

Hand-made felt was made with three strips of knitted wire embedded in the last stages of the felting process. Hand-made braid was used to stitch three panels of knitted wire to the felt between the embedded strips. Before stitching, cords were wrapped around the knitted panels and tied. Beetle-wing decorations were stitched to the ends of the cords.

Lutradur panel

This panel takes its design from a vintage-style decorative paper and incorporates heat-treated copper wire mesh and painted Lutradur 70. The finished panel bears little resemblance to the original design but a shadow of it can be seen through the copper wire mesh.

Design © The Vintage Workshop

Materials

Vintage-style decorative paper

A4 sheet of photocopier paper

A4 size piece of Lutradur 70

Spiral design rubber stamp

Pink and purple chalk inkpads

Heat-treated copper wire mesh, 16 x 20cm (6¼ x 7¾in)

Heat gun

Respirator mask and tongs

Silver and black variegated metallic machine embroidery thread

Small, metallic coloured beads

Fabric scissors

Ruler or tape measure

Sewing needle

1. To create the design on the prepared Lutradur, start by photocopying part of a vintage-style decorative paper, or an enlarged section of it, on to an A4 sheet of paper. If required, alter the colour on the computer, having scanned in the original decorative paper. Copy this image on to an A4 size sheet of Lutradur 70 by placing the Lutradur in the paper tray of the photocopier. The photocopy ink will fade slightly when the Lutradur is left in daylight. The result will be an 'abstract' version of the original design. Cut this down to a piece measuring 11 x 20cm (4¼ x 7¾in), having determined the best area to be used for your work.

2. Press the rubber stamp firmly on to the pink and purple chalk inkpads and transfer the design to the Lutradur. Repeat this several times to create a regular pattern.

3. Using the same colours, create the same pattern on the heat-treated copper wire mesh.

4. Using free machining, stitch around the outer edges of the spirals on the Lutradur with a silver and black variegated metallic machine embroidery thread.

5. Heat the Lutradur carefully and slowly until it just begins to shrink and create a lacy effect. Hold the Lutradur with a pair of tongs and wear a respirator mask to protect yourself from the slightly toxic fumes this may produce. The size of the Lutradur after heat treatment should be reduced to 9.5 x 17cm (3¾ x 6¾in).

6. Lay the heat-treated Lutradur in the centre of the copper wire mesh and attach the two layers together by sewing a small, metallic coloured bead in the centre of each spiral.

7. Cut a section from the original decorative paper the same size as the copper wire mesh and lay the decorated panel over the top of it. The panel can then be mounted or framed as required.

The completed Lutradur panel.